How was this Universe formed? What lies outside of this Universe? What is your true purpose on Earth? Where did you come from before you began life on Earth? What other kinds of Beings exist outside of this World, this Universe?

What kind of a Man was Jesus? And was he anti-religious? Is it true that highly Intelligent Beings watch this Earth closely now, ready to communicate? What is the key that will trigger off the unimaginable Powers lying dormant in each of Man? What is the fact, not theory, about other highly advanced civilisations that existed many thousands of years ago?

Only a Man of all times, all places, all ways of life, could answer those questions with authority and certainty. A Being who was present when all those events took place, a Being from outside of this Universe, and yet one who has lived within it.

Just such a Being does exist. Just such a Being relayed the words of Pure Intelligence contained within these pages – through the pen of one who is as you. A Being, to whom no mystery exists, inspired the answers to all of these questions, and many more.

You too, can become a Man Inspired, with a direct link to the Source of All Intelligence – simply. Inspiration is not for the privileged few – Inspiration is for All.

Read on, for the answer to **your** questions.

INSPIRATION...
IS FOR ALL

penned by
BILL DAWSON

POWER PUBLISHING (U.K.) LTD.

First published in 1978 by Power Publishing (U.K.) Ltd.
Brockwell Cottage, Sowerby Bridge, West Yorkshire
HX6 3PQ. Telephone Halifax (0422) 31013

The Author of this book would welcome
communication with readers, and may be
contacted via the Publishers.
The same applies to other Authors who
have books in this series.
(Please send s.a.e. for reply).

ISBN 0 906220 04 1

Printed and bound in U.K. by
C. Nicholls & Company Ltd
The Philips Park Press, Manchester

The Author of the words which follow is not the 'I' which writes them down by hand, but rather a Being of which I am an extension – a Being which is all-knowing and whose very existence is Truth, Reality.

Although I am merely the Scribe and not the Author, I stand by, and take responsibilty for, every word I have written.

CHAPTER ONE

You have aliens amongst you now. You do not know it, and yet they are in your offices, shops, schools, factories – even within your government. These "beings" are as you in bodily form and in everyday actions, **but they are not of this Universe.** They are here for one single purpose – to help man to evolve and to bring about an age of wisdom and understanding. They are not here to force themselves upon you in any way whatsoever; that is contrary to their nature. Nor have they any intention of helping those who have no wish to be helped. But here they are and here they stay until they have completed their mission.

They have not yet revealed themselves to you, for the moment was not right, and they themselves, before coming, agreed to be "blanked off" from knowing their true origins so that they may lead a life exactly as man in all respects. But now the moment is here for those beings who, in their man form, are of all ages, all races, all nations, and all walks of life. They are now ready to step forward in the full knowledge of who and what they are, and to begin to give to mankind the benefits of the wisdom and powers which they arranged to have sent to them, by means of thought, at the commencement of their task.

We would not expect man to believe us or to take our words seriously, if we were not able to prove all that we say is Truth, and to show him in a practical way the benefits which we bring him.

Prepare yourself now for an Age of Wonder, an age when man can become a being inspired if he cares to be so. Ahead lies an age of discovery, when man can find out all about himself and his Universe. It is so easy to make prophecies and talk vaguely of things to come in future ages, when all who listen to you will be "dead", as you say. But I say that the age I speak of has now begun and will come to flower during the lifetime of this generation.

I know that many of man will, *at first,* ridicule my words and the words of others of Our Realms as they begin to relay to him the Truth of all, for there have been messengers sent to your Earth many times before in an attempt to bring man to a state of enlightenment, for we truly do care deeply for mankind.

In past civilisations, such ambassadors have sometimes been well received and heeded, before man slipped back once again into a state of ignorance and confusion. At other times they were rejected out of hand, and even, on occasions, man has attacked and even "killed" the bodies that they were using.

In this age you still have free choice to do as you want to do, but if you are wise you will not try to prevent those who come amongst you from going about their affairs of Soul. Nothing can prevent you from annihilation if you take that way.

Occasionally odd ways or words brought by one from Our Realms in an earlier civilisation has drifted down to other ages – but always twisted and put in a religious way. One such word is "Soul". Now the word "Soul" is one of such vast importance of meaning, for in its true sense it contains the answer to the mystery of the Universe itself. First it is necessary to be absolutely clear that Soul does not in any way signify what religion teaches – that it is some small item existing within each body of man, which goes to some fairy land or hell when the body dies.

A Soul is such a mighty being of radiance, wisdom and beauty. It is made up of Power and Intelligence and it contains the very Essence of Life. Each Universe has **one** Soul only, and it is controlled by that Soul absolutely. A Soul has the capacity to take a part of itself and to divide up that part into millions of smaller parts. It gives to those "Soulparts", in a very minute degree, the very Essence of which its own Self is made. It gives them a free choice of action, although they are constantly linked to the Soul for as long as they remain Soulparts of that Soul.

It then places these beings, which are in reality its Self, on the Earth of its own Universe. There they are given a task to perform for their Soul, and a chance to begin to evolve on their own account.

In each Universe there are many millions of "realms", which lie between the first stepping-stone of Earth and the seat of the Soul itself, at the very head of the Universe.

Each Soulpart is given the opportunity to move forever higher and higher up through the realms of the Universe through a process of evolving. This is a means of earning a higher state of Power and Intelligence, until it reaches the realm next to the very Soul of the Universe – a state so highly developed as to be almost as the Soul itself. From there, if it cares to do so, the Soulpart may, by performance of special service to its Soul, be given the necessary Essence to take over a Universe and become a Soul in its own right.

It will then have the capacity, for the first time, to take a part of Self and divide it into "beings" which are Soulparts, as it once was itself. These it places on the Earth of its own Universe, and so begins again that part of the cycle of evolution. Many Soulparts prefer to remain in the realms of their own Soul and enjoy to the full the benefits of all that they have earned by their evolving.

Now you have the basis of understanding of who you are and of your purpose in life. Allow me to explain further. Each and every one of you of mankind is a Soulpart of the Soul of this Universe. You are a part of the very Being which is the

Intelligence of this Universe. You are on this Earth to carry out the two-fold purpose of earning for your Soul and of beginning to evolve personally for your self.

It was originally intended that you complete your task during just one brief life on Earth, but most of mankind of today has had to come back to Earth time and time again just to complete that one task. Each time he fails he returns to the temporary home of a "Transit Realm" for a short rest before he starts out again with the full intention of returning to Earth to fulfil his task. But upon arrival once again upon this Planet, so great is the indoctrination pressed upon him from all sides that once more he is taken away from his purpose. In fact, he then no longer knows what his purpose is.

It is the law of the Universe that no Soulpart can pass on to enjoy the Realms of Soul until he has fulfilled his task on Earth. Some of man have had as many as thousands of lives, trying to achieve the same objective.

This now raises the questions of why man has no recollection of who he is or of any past life on Earth – and also of why he does not retain any memory of what is his purpose in life. It seems to be unfair to expect any being to carry out a task if he is not allowed to know what that task is.

In answer to the first question, I say that the state of being, even in the temporary "Transit Realms" is on such a high level of peace and happiness and enjoyment that to be able to recall it whilst on the Earth Plane, where all is at present so ugly and full of sadness and viciousness, would make your life totally unbearable. It would be too cruel. To recall earlier lives spent on Earth would serve no purpose.

To answer the last part of the question, regarding the unfairness of expecting a being to perform a task he is not allowed to know about, I must tell you about how all was intended to be by Soul – in fact, how things were during the first million years of man's existence.

In this Universe, thought is the means of communication used by Soul and Soulparts. It is the natural way to be, so that when man first arrived on Earth he was in constant two-way contact with his Soul by thought. Soul sent man guidance and understanding concerning all things necessary for his requirements and for the fulfilling of his purpose. Man talked to his Soul constantly in his thoughts, and in so doing he was in perfect harmony with all other beings upon the Earth, and with the whole Universe. All went so well, so easily, and man enjoyed all that Soul put there for him. He needed but one short, happiness-crammed life on Earth to earn for himself a permanent home in the high realms of Soul. Soul was satisfied, and no return to Earth was necessary.

There came a time when the emotion of *greed* (of wanting that little bit more than was provided) crept in, and that caused other ugly emotions to follow. Bit by bit the communication with his Soul was neglected by man, because in certain matters he did not want to listen to the guidance given by his greater Intelligence – Soul. In these respects, their children and children's children were taught to act in the same greedy ways, instead of listening to their own Soul direct.

Gradually, over a period of thousands and thousands of years, the voice of man teaching his children how to behave grew louder than the voice of Soul within. In time, because man did not like to change from the way he was, he devised a system of organised teaching of all the new arrivals upon Earth (his children) the right and wrong way to act as man saw fit – not as the Universal Intelligence would guide them in thought.

The downward way of man took place about four million years ago. In your present age, the organised teaching (indoctrination as it really is) in schools, churches and homes, as well as through broadcasting, is so complete that no new-comer to Earth has any hope of avoiding bowing down before it. No one is allowed, let alone encouraged, to listen to and follow the voice of his own Soul, even though Soul is constantly trying to impress him in thought with the right way to go.

Yes, man is persistently being told by Soul of his purpose in life, of the way required to fulfil his task – but so total is the present way of indoctrination from birth till death, that it completely blocks him from hearing the Universal Soul in any way. He has now become a being trying to live without the use of his natural Intelligence. Pathetically he scrabbles for knowledge and an understanding of life, with the test tube of the scientist and the rituals of religion, when all could be his for the asking. He complains he has not been allowed (perhaps by his particular God) to know the purpose of life, when all the time he blocks the voice of the Intelligence of the Universe that would tell him – Soul.

It is the Code of Souls that all Soulparts have free choice of the way that they wish to go – the way of value of Soul or the way of no value, the way of selfishness. If this were not so, then evolution would not be possible – and all beings must evolve, one way or another. During the last four million years the Soul of this Universe has been trying to get man to complete his task of his own free choice, but now time is running out for man, and for his Universe. Because of the way man is, this Universe is about to collapse in upon itself.

All things within Existence are either growing or decaying, and your Universe is no exception. Other Universes are pressing in upon it as they expand and already it is considerably smaller under the pressure that it cannot resist because of lack of Power. It is rather like a building block which is crumbling and cannot withstand the pressure of all those upon it. It has to be knocked out and replaced so as not to cause the collapse of all those depending upon it.

The purpose of man upon his Earth is to help produce Power for his own Universe, his own Soul.

All Universes must produce their own Power in order to continue to exist. Each Universe contains many, many planets but only one Earth – only the one planet which is capable of producing Power to maintain that Universe. Earth is the dynamo of the Universe, but yours has almost ceased producing Power during the last four million years. It is this that I came to tell you of – *to warn you about*.

My mission is to tell you, in a simple way, exactly how things are with you in relation to your Earth and Universe and Purpose, then to point the way you must go to put matters right, if you care to do so.

I have no intention of criticising you in any way, and your decision to rectify matters or to carry on as you are towards your own annihilation cannot affect myself, or any other from the lands of Soul. Soul will act to see that no other Universe suffers because of the folding in of this one, if that becomes necessary. The choice is with man entirely.

CHAPTER TWO

At this point in time, there are billions upon billions of Universes. A man would not be able to count them all in one lifetime. This Universe of yours is so tiny compared with others which are a million times larger in volume. Imagine if you can, therefore, the extent of such an area of Space that would be neccessary to contain them all. An area so vast as to baffle the imagination of man. This is what we refer to as the Lands of Soul.

Originally before the beginning of time or Universes, before Soul existed even, there was only this vast, empty Space, and within it there lay the Mass of Power.

The Mass of Power existed – without movement, without consciousness of Self. It remained so over countless eons of ages – as a speck within a vast sea of apparent nothingness. Then, without knowing exactly when, the Mass of Power was conscious of existing. It became aware of Self but did not know what Self was, or what anything was, for there was nothing but Self. Thus it remained for other ages longer, unmoving, merely aware of existing.

During a period of looking into Self, the Mass of Power accidentally triggered off a movement. It knew now that it could move, and searched until it again found the source of the movement. It moved again, changing positions endlessly – at first jerkily and unexpectedly, then later smoothly and in a more controlled manner.

The Mass that was Power then looked outside of Self, and saw – nothing. Nothing, that is, except a seemingly endless expanse of substance in all directions. The Mass realised for the first time that it was "alone". So it remained for further ages, as the sense of being alone grew and grew within it.

The sense of utter loneliness drove it to a state of movement to begin to search the volume of nothingness that lay around it, to discover if there might be another such thing as its Self.

It passed more eons searching all of that area, but found in the end nothing but the substance which filled it. With this realisation the loneliness within became an agony – a sense of utter despair.

But during all the experimentation with himself, and the searching without, the Mass that was Power discovered one all-important item. It found, within itself, that Essence which is Intelligence. This discovery did not come easily or quickly for it meant recognising the pattern of Intelligence within the complex, pulsing, seething Mass that was Self.

The Mass was not Power alone, but Power and Intelligence combined.

The Mass of Power then decided, under the guidance of Intelligence, that if it could not discover another outside of Self to dispel that awful agony of loneliness, then it would create another from the very Power that was Self. And thus began long eons of experiments. Trial and error. There was no other way it could be.

Imagine a very wise old man, sitting there looking out at nothingness, entirely surrounded by nothingness, with no experience of anything other than himself – trying to visualise how all could be. Such was the condition of the Mass of Power.

First it discussed within itself, and then the Power, under the guidance of Intelligence, took small fragments of itself and placed them upon its outer perimeter. These pieces immediately began to disintegrate, to mingle with the substance of Space to become as nothing. Each time this experiment was repeated, the same thing occurred – the lumps of the Mass just melted into the substance around them. The Mass of Power then realised that any creature formed would have to be placed inside the boundary of the Mass itself. So more random shapes of pieces of the Mass were placed on its outer rim, but this time within a skin of protection. These lumps remained sitting there, exactly where they were placed, able to serve no purpose. They were withdrawn, and again the Mass reconsidered the problem. When next they were left to drift free within a substance-filled area within the Mass, they merely drifted and banged against each other and substance, until they all became more smooth and rounded – but still there was no purposeful action.

Eons of ages passed, and many more shapes and sizes were tried, but always they were drawn in as being unsatisfactory. The Wise Old Man that was the Mass went on and on, never once having the thought that there might not be a way. Trial and error, trial and error. *The Power combined with the Intelligence would find a way.*

So weird and unsightly were many of the beings created, for there had been nothing before to guide the Mass to copy from. Some were snakey in shape, some spikey, some flat, some round. Some of the first ones were so disastrous, for they were made with Power without the corresponding Intelligence, and the only result was violence and chaos. Quickly they had to be folded-in, and a new start made. Eventually, the prototype of the first successful species of being was arrived at.

In its original state it was so crude in shape and clumsy of movement, but to the Mass of Power it was beautiful, magnificent – *for it served the purpose for which it was created.*

As well as being the answer to the problem of the terrible loneliness of the Mass, it was the first being created which was able to make additional Power, of which the Mass of Power required a new continuous supply, in order to be able to use it to make other beings.

That first being was one of the species which you of man call "Bird".

I will tell you now about the first successful prototype of being created by the Mass. And by successful I mean one which had the capacity to fulfil satisfactorily the purpose for which it was created. A being can have no greater success than to fulfil its own destiny. Any other way which it takes can only mean failure and non-evolvement – as is the case with man at present.

In the very early stages, when the created beings were still unsightly lumps in shape, the Ultimate made an Earth to use as a base for them to move about upon. Then they were made to hop, and eventually jump higher and still higher. Matters really began to progress after the bone structure had been improved and made light, strong, and flexible. After another period of trial and error, Soul made them able to stay off the ground for longer periods whilst going forward through the substance surrounding the surface of the Earth. Flight of a sort had been achieved.

After further experimentation, the ungainly ones began to move more gracefully, but it was discovered that any prolonged movement through the substance called "air", chilled the body of these creatures. Gruesome in shape though they may have been in the first stages, they were not just lumps of lifeless clay, but warm, living, breathing, throbbing, delicate and complex beings – ones with awareness and feeling.

So various types of covering were arranged and tried and tested, as were many ways of attaching the covering. Soul then came to the understanding that the creature could be made to grow its own covering from within itself – and this method worked very well. And so the beings became feathered.

The next problem that arose was what man would call "refuelling in flight", if applied to his flying machines. Because the birdlike ones were required to move swiftly over long distances through the substance "air" without having to stop and land to find food and eat it, a method of feeding as they were flying became necessary. As a result, once again, of trial and error, this time with various species of insects, a colony of tiny flies was produced which served the purpose admirably.

Various other alterations, amendments, and improvements were carried out, and the ages passed quickly, so that it was long eons before the first satisfactory prototype was ready to populate the first Universe of Soul. This final "model" differed from all the others, when it was accomplished, in that it was the first being made which had the capacity, the means, *to Power its own Soul.*

The Bird was a truly glorious being for Soul, for not only did it have finally beauty of shape, grace of movement, but *it fulfilled all that was required of it by its Creator,* and it had become the means of the expansion of the Universe, the converting of the substance of Space to Power, which was to be used for the benefit of all within the Mass of Power.

Many types of being were made after this, beings that man can have no conception of, for he has not the capacity to comprehend that which is not within his own Universe – and even that which is, he often does not bother to truly observe, so obsessed with self and that which he imagines might serve his selfishness.

But you, my scribe, have been taught by me to observe many things afresh, to look at all from the point of view of Soul, not the point of view of self, as you were previously accustomed to doing when you lived and thought as man does.

All the beings on this Earth are prototypes. Each species was created separately and has its own Universe. Each type, even, of what you regard as species, had its own Universe, for it was created separately. Of any two, even slightly differing types of animal or bird or insect – no one has "evolved" from another. Each is a prototype. Each is as it is, as it was when it was when it was created in a separate instance by Soul. There is no such thing as evolution on an Earth – by one type or species of being gradually changing into another. This just is not so, it is not in accordance with facts or reality.

Sometimes, after a period of years on this Earth, Soul rests some species of being by withdrawing them, and replacing them with prototypes from other Universes close by – but never, never does one species change itself into another. It is not possible.

I realise that you, my scribe, already know of this, for I have given you an insight into the way of Soul, but I repeat it as a means of your bringing it to the attention of man, for he is now so befuddled with the "experts" theories of evolution, that he really does not know if the animals are coming or going, or if indeed they have ever "come" at all – from Soul.

Look at a popular domestic animal the Cat. See how many different types that there are, within that one species, and yet not one of these types evolved from another. Each type within a species, not just each species, had its own Universe, each type that you see on Earth is a separately modelled prototype of its kind. So many, so many. The same goes for all other animals and insects, as well as birds. Man has on his Earth the representatives of thousands upon thousands of Universes – all trying to do their part to help man to fulfil his task, his purpose in life.

Allow me to guide you to observe, anew, the Bird as it is upon this Earth, and to show you how superior it is to the protype of being that is man.

Look at the beak of a Bird. It uses it to clean itself, very efficiently and without fuss, or the use of any other articles. Man cannot do this. The Bird uses the beak to feed himself, to break up, to select, to carry his food. Man cannot do this. The Bird can dig with its beak. He can build his home with his beak, in some cases even cement it together. He can feed his

19

young with his beak, and catch flying insects in the air whilst travelling at high speeds. He uses it to increase his speed of flight by parting the substances with his beak. He can do so many things with that one single item that man cannot do without an elaborate system of implements, if at all.

Look at the foot of the Bird. So delicately formed, yet spreading out so as to balance the creature at many extreme angles, so made as to grip many varying thicknesses and textures. They hold a Bird firm in the middle of high winds, and in exposed positions. With his feet the Bird is able to patter along the ground and so attract certain insects to come to the surface. Of these insects he selects only what was put there for him, leaving the rest – content to take only that which Soul put there for him alone.

How unlike man, with his greed and grasping – how superior to man.

How slender are the legs, and yet of such strength. They easily support the weight of the body of the Bird when landing at high speed, when running and jumping – and Birds can jump very high indeed, as you will see if you watch them when playing. Birds do play often, even when you may think that they are quarrelling and fighting. They have a great sense of fun and enjoyment. You can only see a Bird take on the emotion of anger on a very rare occasion indeed – but when they do for that moment turn from Soul – they kill.

How unlike man with his jealousies and angers and hatreds, fightings, wars and constant killings – how superior by far.

Study the feather formation of the Bird. So warming, so protective, so proof against rain – each feather perfectly in place, one overlapping the other all over the contours of the body. The whole of them built to take into account the wind resistance, the balance of flight, manoeuvrability in the air – each wing and tail feather placed exactly for this purpose.

Study the language of Birds – see how they use the voice to

sing, laugh, chatter. But look closer and see how they communicate with the complex language of movement. The set of the head, the attitude of the body, the stance, the movement of the tail, the wings, feathers.

How hoarse and harsh is the voice of man, the way he uses it, for he shows all his hateful and negative emotions in his voice.

But above all, Birds fulfil their purpose of Soul. They all complete their task, they make Power for the Soul – when man allows. They listen constantly to their Soul, and they follow the guidance of Soul – what man in his ignorant way calls "instinct".

For some, Soul tells them where he has prepared supplies of food for them, and so they gather together in large numbers and fly off at regular intervals to those selected areas. They choose leaders, usually ones who have made the journey before, and each Bird remains behind its selected leader. The leader always remains in front, none overtakes. The leader selects certain ones to keep watch on the stragglers, to drop back and gather them together and guide them to their destination – all under the overall guidance of Soul.

What a wonderful example are these creature of grace and beauty and efficiency – each caring for the other in a good way.

None imprisoning or encroaching upon the other in any way, as is the case with man.

The couples have young, rear them, feed and look after them with caring and attention, until the moment when they are able to fend for themselves, under the guidance of Soul, or "instinct" as man calls it. Then they leave them free to follow their own lives, to fulfil their purpose in life. No strings, no obligations, no restrictions – such as man imposes on his young.

How superior to man is the Bird, in this one all-important aspect of listening to Soul and fulfilling its task in life. This, in the eyes of Soul, in the eyes of all the Universes, makes the creature that is Bird, such a Glorious Being, so radiant in Soul, so beloved of the Ultimate, the Creator of All.

But man – what of man? Where is *his* Glory? He has none in any eyes but his own, and they see only self.

But how does man treat these beings who, in Soul home, are a million times more evolved than man, whose wisdom and might make the puny way of man seem as nought, but who come in gentleness and grace to help the lowly prototype that is man to fulfil his own Universe – how does he treat them?

He uses them. Some, who please him in colour or in song, he imprisons for the whole of their lives in a tiny cage, often so that they can never use their limbs at all, their wings, –rather like a man being always in a cage, so small that he can never walk during the whole of his life on Earth. But worse than this, *man prevents the Bird,* by his imprisonment, *from carrying out the task he came to do* – and so he has to come again and spend another life in this place – made so ugly and filthy by man.

Or others of man may merely shoot at him with weapons of hate, for their personal enjoyment and perverted satisfaction in maiming and killing these gentle creatures of Soul. Afterwards they may gorge themselves upon the dead carcass – to further their enjoyment.

Man may even arrange competitions with prizes for thinking up the most efficient way of murdering the friendly and gentle Birds who live upon the buildings in large cities – for the best way of slaughtering them, so that their droppings do not spoil the great beauty of the city buildings.

Man buys and sells these beings, imprisons them, kills them for pleasure, slaughters them en-masse when they inconvenience him, sprays with insecticides, "breeds" them for money, and eats their dead bodies.

Man, the first, undeveloped, degenerated prototype of his species – the lowest of the low, the dregs of the Universes, the thwarter of his own Soul, the cancer that eats at the insides of the Power that is the Mass – this one has the gall and the arrogance to treat thus those who are his superiors in every way, the evolved ones of Soul.

What utter stupidity – what horror.

But this way of mal-treatment that man has, this utter disregard for, this making use of beings who are millions of times more evolved in their own Universes – it is not restricted only to Birds of flight, but to all other creatures which man encounters on this Earth of his. He has complete and utter disregard for ought but self.

Just a glance briefly at his treatment of *any creature,* animal, bird or insect, shows man for what he is. Man thinks them inferior to him. Poor misguided fool. Only his own arrogance, his own blown-up vision of Self, prevents him from seeing others as they really are.

My scribe, his own Soul bears the shame for him, his own Soul suffers for him, his own Soul would dearly love to be able to pay back for him, for all the evils and atrocities committed by man of his own Universe. But the Ultimate, the Creator of All, will not permit this – nor is it possible within the Code of Souls.

Each and every one must pay in detail and depth for every single action committed against another (whether seen or unseen by his fellow man). Every evil perpetrated against his superiors, the Evolved Ones, helps to build up that debt. All must pay – all. No single being escapes one single act of evil, in any way. The Soul of All says so.

But most of all, most important of all actions – he who prevents any other being from carrying out its task, be it animal, bird, insect or man, – then he pays and pays and pays, both on this Earth and in Soul. There is no escape. In doing such a thing he is setting himself against Soul – the Might and Power of Soul – the Plan, the Purpose of Soul – of the Ultimate.

Dear scribe, it would be more than you could bear in your present state, for me to show you but one small glimpse of the Voids of this Universe, overcrowded with such evil ones. I command you to tell man of his own ways, of what he does – and of the consequences.

The burden of the evil and futility that man is causing, lies heavy upon Soul, and unless he immediately will change his ways and cure himself, the cancer that is man will with certainty have to be cut out, before it can eat out the heart of the Universes that are Soul.

You cannot impress upon him often enough, or strongly enough, that *the choice is man's – change or extinction.*

CHAPTER THREE

Many of man speak of mysteries – the mystery of the Universe, the mystery of life, the mystery of death, of other civilisations, of the Earth, of your various Gods. Notice that it is mostly your experts in the fields of science, religions and art who invent these so-called mysteries – and it is not to be wondered at, for "mystery" is merely a word to cover up a state of ignorance on any particular matter.

There is no such thing as a mystery, for Soul has an understanding of all things. In fact, every item and circumstance within all the Universes is arranged by Soul, in exactly the way that it occurs. All the basic items of the Universe, and many more outside of it, are explainable in simple terms, for Truth is simple – it is only lies and inventions which need to be complex.

How old is your Earth? Or other planets, or even the Universe? Your men of science, who claim to be experts in such things say that the Earth is about 4,500 million years old, and they claim to know this by measuring the rate of decay of certain substances within soil or rock, and other such means.

Some religious leaders quote what unknown writers state in fragments of ancient scripts – that it is about five thousand years old, or twenty five thousand and so on. All of these self-styled experts are believed by large groups of people – and believed blindly, for who is there to disprove them?

I will tell you the true age of this Earth and all the planets and stars – the age of the whole Universe, for all came into being at the same moment. I know, for the simple reason that I was there at that moment – I assisted in the forming of it. I am Soul, and I had the honour to be present when the Soul of this Universe was made from a Soulpart into the status of a Soul in its own right. I was present when it received that certain Essence from the Core of the Mass of Power, which would enable it to divide up a part of its Self and form beings to populate its own newly formed Universe.

That moment occurred five million years ago, reckoned in your Earth time. Every particle of dust or gas or liquid throughout the whole of the Universe is exactly the same age – every scrap of rock on your Earth is the same age. It could not be otherwise.

Some scientists tell us in great detail of the why's and where-fore's of various stars, which they say are merely other "Suns" – yet they claim that these "Suns" are so far away that their light takes millions of years to reach Earth.

I tell you now that stars are not "Suns", nor have they ever been. Listen carefully as you read my words following, and you will be more knowledgeable of Truth than all the astronomers of the world put together. They can tell you only the results of their vague theories, but I tell you how all is, as I view it at this moment.

The shape of the Universe is that of a cone standing on end, or the spiral of a coiled spring. The whole area of what you can see, including what you call the stars, planets, sun, moon and earth, is situated within the tiniest portion at the very "base" or tip of the cone.

The Sun is situated, as I have mentioned, at the very base of the spiral that is this Universe. It is there to divide off what I call dross – rubbish of substance – from the true Essence of Soul. It blocks the way from all the true substances that go to make Soul, and it keeps below it at the base of the cone, all the beings who have no desire to do their task below and make, in a way, all of Eternity easier for not only themselves but all of their Soul.

Below the Sun there is the Earth. Now it is a mistaken idea

to say that the Earth goes "around" the Sun. It does not. Try to visualise an invisible cord joining the Earth to the Sun (with the Earth hanging below). Then give the Earth a push so that it swings from side to side like a pendulum, but so that it swings out a little to the side each time, in a sort of "Squashed in" circle, an ellipse. Then that is the motion of the Earth. It also turns as it swings, but, so gently.

Now of the billions of lighted objects that you see in the sky, some of them are planets and the others are merely guiding lights, or beacons marking entry to the transit realms of Soul.

There is only one Sun. All of the planets you see in the sky are positioned "below" the Earth in the curved tip of the cone. That is the reason that you can only see them at night-time, that is, when part of the Earth that you are on is facing away from the Sun and towards the base of the Universe.

The Moon, about which man now imagines that he knows so much, is *not* a satellite of Earth. In fact it traces a spiralling path between the outer rim of the "atmosphere" of Earth and the nearest planets.

I realise that all this is entirely different from all the present-day theories you have had fed into your minds from the moment of starting school – theories presented as fact. Almost all of "civilised" man has been "forcibly fed" with the fashionable scientific theories of the day – as if they were proven truths. But I tell you how things are in reality – and soon I prove all my words beyond a shadow of a doubt.

Nothing in the Universe is random – nothing happens by chance. There is a very vital reason why all should be positioned as it is, and that can be summed up in the one word – *Power*.

The only reason man needs to be on Earth at all is this – *to earn Power for his Soul*. If it were not for this necessity, then each Soulpart would be able to go straight to his permanent home in the Soul Realms, and begin evolving in his own right. But the whole Universe is designed as one great Power-making machine. It works like this –

Each Soulpart, as he arrives on Earth, is given a machine to take care of. It is a Power-producing machine, and it is very simple to operate. The raw material is fed into one end, the machine automatically processes it, and outputs the finished product. That machine is what man refers to as the body. Some of man even go so far as to think that they *are* the machine.

The Output from the body machine should naturally go directly into the ground. It is in the form of highly concentrated soil, and when mixed with other soil it soon breaks down, and is acted upon by a minute form of life which converts it into another form. The Output usually goes through a process of peat, coal, oil and gas – each stage being a natural processing of the Power-making machine that is the Earth.

Consider the body! The body of Bird, Insect and Animal, as well as the body of man. What superb Intelligence has been at work to design a machine so well as to have thousands of moving living parts – so precise in every detail, each part fitting perfectly with every other. Nothing left to chance. Some can burrow in the ground, float in the air, or cleave through the water. And yet man cannot construct even one tiny microbe or piece of living flesh from any one of these wondrous bodies. The Intelligence of the designer obviously must exceed the total Intelligence used by all of man. – By a least a million times.

Yet let us consider one particular aspect of the body. Man says that food is taken in at the mouth, processed so that the body can use it to sustain itself, and the remainder is output as waste. Now why should an Intelligence, a million times superior to man, having designed such a marvellous living machine, make it so imperfect as to be able to make use of only a small proportion of the food imput? It is true that man does not eat the natural food for which the machine is designed – but can the same be said of every single wild animal and bird and insect on this Earth?

No, it cannot be so, even using man's logic. To have a computerised (with brain), fully automatic processing, self-maintaining, living machine – and then to have it Outputting waste matter for no good reason – this would be to make the Intelligence which designed it into an idiot. Also, to have such complex, precision machines merely for housing a mind, or a brain, is not feasible either.

The reality of the situation is this – that the body of man (as well as animals, etc), is a machine made with the intention of producing a finished article – as you have in your factories. On being supplied with imput materials (food) it carries out a complex processing of the imput, and then it produces what man refers to as excretia and urine, or "Output" as I shall refer to it.

I realise that in this present civilisation the Output of the body of man is regarded as smelly and unpleasant and disease-ridden, and I agree with him that it is so at present. You see, when the materials put into a machine are not the ones intended for processing in that machine, then the product Output from it will not be as the designer intended it should be.

For instance, if you insert minced-up dead bodies of animals into a machine, what can the Output be expected to be like, but smelly and unpleasant and disease-ridden? But with an animal which is allowed to eat its natural food the result is quite different. Some of your most prized and expensive perfumes come from the intestines of the whale and other animals – so you can imagine how the Output of man could be, if he cared to make it so by correct eating habits.

So each one of you of mankind is in possession of a wonder machine – a machine not just wonderful because of the in-

29

genious way of its design and functioning, but because of the Output which it can produce, which could be the source of *Power* for the Soul of this Universe.

That is your task in life, your purpose for living upon this Earth – *to produce Power for your own Soul.*

And all you need to do is to stop placing pieces of the dead bodies of your fellow beings into the machine, and place your Output directly into the Earth and cover it immediately with soil. Nothing more and nothing less. The natural way of the Earth would then take over and complete the process, which would turn the Output into a pure form of Power ready to be used by Soul to Power the Universe. At the same time the soil substances would nourish the Earth ready for your seedlings to benefit from. If you eat animals your Output must stay in the Earth longer, before the way of the animal substances dissolves.

What I have just told you may seem very difficult for you to accept, for such has been the indoctrination of man, especially in the more "advanced" countries, that he even shies away from discussing the subject of Output, or effluence. There are many of the more crude-minded ones who will snigger and make coarse jokes about it in an offensive way, but I do not intend to be offensive in any way – merely to place the facts before you as they are.

After all, it is not usually considered rude or unpleasant when a farmer says he is "muck-spreading", or fertilising his crops, or when a friend obtains manure to place near his roses. So treat my words seriously as I give them. Consider my words, and when you have looked impartially and unemotionally, listen to the voice of reason within – *then* you will know that I am right, for you will be listening to Soul.

Words are so necessary to man of today, words in sound and words in writing. He needs constant contact with his fellows, and the more complex he makes his life the greater the need for exchange of words, of ideas through words. Without his precious words he would not be able to have "co-operation" in industry and commerce, or to teach others what he claims is right, or fool others into thinking how clever he is, or even to plan his wars or stir up trouble on some larger scale. It is also true that without words he would not be able to be loving or caring or kind to others in the same way, or to enjoy companionship and exchange of ideas.

It was not always so. There was a time when all of man were in full contact with the Universal Intelligence that is their Soul.

By thought, they were guided in all that they did, and because it was the same Intelligence that sent thoughts to all of man, whatever one was guided to do was always in perfect harmony with all others. Words were just not necessary for the harmonising of actions, nor were they necessary for one to try to help another to understanding. Each man was a person inspired and all understood the ways of all others. Soul made it so. This does not mean to say that man did not use words.

It would have appeared to an unknowing alien visitor that they were in contact by what man calls "telepathy", the transferring of thoughts from one mind to another, and in a way he would have been right, for Soul would send thoughts to one to let him know what another wished him to understand – when Soul considered it necessary.

Now I tell you some exciting news! This day could be the beginning of the return to the age of Universal mental contact – a harmonising of minds and actions by thought, through the intermediary of Soul. I say "could be" – if man chooses to have it so.

You could try a little experiment now if you cared to do so. It is quite simple, and requires a little effort on your part, but the reward could be great. If you bring yourself to examine the ideas put before you in this book with a truly open mind – then as you read, your own Soul will relay to you special thoughts of understanding such as you have never experienced before.

By "having an open mind" I mean this – not just examining a new idea and judging it to be true or false according to your own set principles, but examining your set principles and ways placed upon you by your society, in the light of the new idea. Make a real effort to do this impartially and without emotion.

If you do this whilst reading this book, because of a special arrangement with your Soul, a certain channel of your brain will be opened to enable you to receive by direct thought an inspired understanding of at least a part of my words.

I, Soul, will in effect be communicating with you by thought – and *you will know it to be so*. What is more, from that moment your own Soul will begin to care for you in a special way, which you had blocked it from doing before.

Once you have opened up the channel of communication with Soul, you will have become one of the pioneers of the new Age of Enlightenment which now begins. You who read this book, by that one act of courage in opening your mind to *my* way, *will become a leader of mankind*. Only the first few can be leaders – the rest are followers.

Thought is such a powerful thing – once you know how to use it.

Each Universe is made up of substance, matter. Every Universe has a different way of using the Power of Soul to control and arrange that substance, and as a means of communication.

In your Universe the means of controlling all matter and of linking each Soulpart to his Soul – is *thought*. But thought used in the correct way.

On your Earth you have hoards of experts in the ways of thought – specialists who tamper with the brain, and those who try to pry into the mind of man, as well as philosophers who

32

sit and think about thoughts and ways of applying it to living. You have educationists and teachers who try to force thoughts that they consider to be proper into the heads of the young and defenceless of mind.

There are so many of them who gather to themselves wealth and prestige by proclaiming themselves learned in the ways of thought – and yet not one of them really has a true understanding of what a thought is.

First of all, it is assumed that thoughts are made or produced by the brain or mind of man. *This is not so.* No one of man has ever made a thought, for he just is not capable of it. The brain of man, which some refer to as the mind, is merely a receiving set for thoughts which have been sent to it from another source – and that source of all thought is the Soul of the Universe.

From the very moment when a part of the Mass of Soul becomes a being in its own right, a Soulpart, it is linked to the Soul, in the case of this Universe, by means of thought. This link remains for as long as the Soulpart remains within the Universe, and it takes the form of one long, continuous, unbroken stream of thoughts from Soul to being.

Now when the Soulpart arrives on Earth, it is served from Soul by two tracks of thought. One track, which I call the "original" track, serves to feed a stream of "conscious" thoughts to the brain, which are for the considering, and then either rejecting or using.

At the same time, another stream of thoughts is constantly fed along the secondary track, and these are used to control all parts of the body which man regards as working automatically.

For example, a person may be playing a game of cards and talking to his partner. He is receiving thoughts along the original track concerning the value of each card, and after considering each one he uses it to decide how to play that card. He then needs a thought in order to instruct his arm to pick up or put down a card. He also needs to receive thoughts, which he selects before using, in order converse with his partner. All these thoughts are coming along the original track, and according to which one he chooses to use will depend how he acts in mind and body during the game.

At the same time he has an unbroken stream of thoughts flowing to his brain along the secondary track. He is in no way aware of them, for they merely keep his lungs moving, his heart pumping blood around the body, his stomach mechanism digesting the last meal he ate, etc, etc. Each tiniest movement of every organ of the body requires a thought from Soul to the brain. Millions of thoughts pass to the brain for the purpose of just keeping the body working, within the space of one minute – and without the person being aware of it.

Sometimes a person may override the secondary thoughts if he chooses an original thought to do so. For example, his lungs may be working quite normally according to the needs of his body, when he decides to use the thought to do a deep breathing exercise. In this case the original thought takes control from the secondary thoughts, and his lungs begin to go in and out more deeply.

But all man has to be concerned about is the original thought track, for that is the means of his using free choice. He is quite free to choose which thoughts he will accept or reject. He is free to go the right way or go the wrong way. It is quite simple. Man has only the choice of the two ways – the one of value to his task in life, and the way which serves a useless life.

Now if you still believe that you can make a thought, you should be able to say how you make it, and also what gave you the thought to make it. And what about all those thoughts which come "out of the blue", as it seems? Many experts, so-called, because they cannot explain any of the workings of thought or state how you make them or where they come

34

from, invent a word which covers up their ignorance of the matter – they talk of the "subconscious" mind.

They can neither tell you what it is, nor where it is, nor how it is supposed to make a thought – but it helps to confuse an ordinary person who asks a simple question and would expect a simple answer – "What is a thought?".

A thought is a piece of substance, matter. It is real and it is powerful, it can be seen, handled, manipulated by the evolved ones of Soul, though it cannot be seen by man in his present state. Just as the vapour of water often cannot be seen or grasped, and yet when it takes on the form of water or snow or ice, it is easily seen and touched and put into the shape that you wish.

Each thought is substance. The being that is Soul, that is made up of Power and Intelligence, takes a minute part of the Power that is Self, sets it into a pattern with Intelligence, and directs it in a very fine form along a thought track to man. It is so fine that man cannot detect it with any of his senses, but only with that specially sensitive area of his brain which is designed to receive thought.

Thoughts are real, living, substantial things. They are a form of Power and a part of the Soul of this Universe itself. Thoughts are so valuable as well as so Powerful – and yet man wastes them by the million. Such a waste, and yet all the physical items of this Earth could be controlled by thought for the benefit of man. *They were once, and they could be again.*

Man has no need to scrape a miserable living by the sweat of the brow, by labouring long hours, physically and mentally, when he should be enjoying all that is there for him to enjoy – when he takes the right way of thought. How difficult he makes life for himself and for others by doing all in the wrong way – the reverse way.

Thought is so much easier if properly used. It could provide heat and light and shelter for man – *easily*. It could cause the winds and clouds to disappear, and the Earth to be moist without rain. It could cause all the necessary foods to grow where they are required, without your way of spoiling as you do now.

It used to be so once, when man knew the value of thought. Allow those of the realms of Soul to show you how to use the thoughts of value of Soul. But we can only do so if you open your mind to the possibility.

A closed mind is not open to receive value – only the rubbish which man is in the habit of accepting, of selecting.

The choice of one or the other never leaves you.

CHAPTER FOUR

In Soul *you* are gentle. All Souls are gentle. Yet Soul is Power and Intelligence. The Power which is Soul is gentle – but it is irresistible.

Gentleness is the key to much else, to many Soul ways. Practice gentleness at *all* times, on *all* occassions, and see the change that comes about in your life – just through that one change. Gentleness, the quality of Souls, the quality of true Power, irresistible Power.

When you are being gentle in thought you cannot be annoyed, vicious, greedy, selfish, impatient or intolerant – even with yourself. For then you cannot be ungentle in action, or in words.

The *thought* is the thing. Thought controls all. A gentle thought is a mighty thing. It can open all doors – it can find a way where no other kind of thought can.

There was a very gentle person once. He wore gentleness like a cloak. With his gentleness he achieved great things. He did not shout or rave or bluster – he did not thump a pulpit or wave a fist. He did not threaten, or coerce – and yet he had ample Power at his disposal. But he caused thousands upon thousands to listen to his words, to follow his ways.

He told them of Soul – how to understand about their own Soul. He told them gently – he told them to be gentle. He told them of the gentleness of Soul.

His name was Jesus.

I shall tell you the story of Jesus – rather I shall relay to you, the story of Jesus.

It will be the first time the true story of Jesus has been told, has been written. Much has been written about him, much has been written in his name – all of it rubbish – sheer distortion and invention. What you have in the so-called Bible is pure fairy stories. A very, very small percentage is based on fact, but even that has been distorted and twisted.

You know almost nothing of the real Jesus or of his times, or of his travels. What now is to be related to you will astound you – but it is Truth, Truth Supreme. What is now relayed is in the words of Jesus himself, as he speaks them. Let none deny it, for it shall be proved, proved beyond doubt.

*　*　*　*　*

"This is my story. I am he who is known to you as Jesus. You do not know me, no, not at all. All the things, the stories that you have been told about me are mostly untrue. They were written down by "Scribes", men of Religion. Men with vested interests. Men who wrote down some scraps they had heard of me and invented the rest to suit their own purposes. A Religion. Then many religions were made out of my supposed words, and my invented life-story.

I came to destroy religion. To tell man of his Soul, his own Wondrous Soul. I came to lead him away from the un-Soul-like ways of his day. From greed, cruelty, brutality, materialism, superstition, and most of all, religion.

I spoke out against all religions. I came not to make a new one. But man was determined to go his own way, and even some of those from our Soul Lands who came to help, became contaminated and set in the evil ways of man. The few of us who tried to carry out our task were not strong enough to combat the combined evil of man.

Materialism! Religion! The twin curses of man.

I came to teach gentleness and tolerance. Religion, in my name, has taught brutality, cruelty, intolerance and hatred.

I came to teach a simple life. Religion, in my name, has taught pomp and ceremony, riches and luxury and fine robes for the perpetrators of religion.

I came to teach man how to find his own Soul, to be guided by his own Soul in all his thoughts and actions. Religion has taught, in my name, to follow the doctrines of self-appointed leaders and "holy" men, to obey their rules and regulations, to believe that it is wrong to "think for one's self".

I came to teach man all about his own Wonderful Soul – a being of Might and Radiance, Wisdom and Intelligence of which they are a part. A Being caring for them always.

Religion has taught, in my name, that the Soul is some small organ or intangible object at or near the heart, within the body of each man, something which you can blacken or whiten according to your "sins", something so weak and insignificant that priests in fancy dress must chant and pray for, when the owner has "died".

But from this moment forward no longer will man be able to impose his own way, his own rules and regulations on to others, and use my name to do so – or the names of any other so-called prophets or gods. Soul brings to man now a way of knowing, understanding about the whole of this Universe, a way of communicating direct with the very Intelligence that is the Soul of the Universe.

The way shown to you by Soul, and proved to you beyond all doubts by those sent from Soul, will cause all books and bibles and agents of the various so-called gods to be unnecessary and useless – will show them to be the lies that they are.

Once before I came to destroy religion and to replace it with Truth. Now other special ones from other Universes come to do the same thing.

Whose side would you have taken at the time of my last coming to your Earth? Whose side will you take this time?

You, as they of old, may choose.

Know that I come with those Wondrous Souls and parts from the Core of All. Will you treat me again as you did before?"

* * * * *

I speak to you now of one who was known in the times of Jesus, as Simon of Egypt. There are many Soulparts from those days who are waiting to relay their stories of Truth through scribes placed on Earth for just that purpose. What follows now is in the words of Simon himself.

* * * * *

I will tell you now of one of my lives, in Egypt. I was a young man at the time, a young man of ability. I had a flair for teaching others and for organising this teaching. I thought to put this ability to good use with the youth of my society. I had already tried out the scheme in a very limited fashion, and knew with certainty that I had developed a wonderful, simple teaching and learning system.

Even though I had received an advanced education, I was of low birth, and during the course of my day-time work I was sent to deliver some articles to the Great Palace – the centre of culture and rule in the land of Egypt, in the north.

I entered and completed my lowly task, and found myself asked to wait in a certain lavish, vaulted chamber. I stood back amongst the many religious and secular dignitaries who were standing around in groups discussing. I felt honoured to be in such a place, and was prepared to leave at any moment.

I was amazed when some of the high officials began to

gently draw me into conversation, to ask my opinions, almost to treat me as one of themselves. But still I did not realise that the whole thing had been planned. I was too overwhelmed by all the pomp and magnificence, and the great honour that these men were doing me.

Then there was a movement near the "top-end" of the chamber (shaped like the prow of a boat). A door opened between two great pillars, and out stepped the Great Leader himself. One who was feared and held in awe and wonder throughout the land. The magnificence of his attire was both astounding and dazzling. No dress or robes have ever been so glorious or superb in the present era. I who was used to the pomp and extravagance of Egypt, was quite stunned by his appearance.

Then, to utterly confound me, this Prince came straight forward and greeted me almost as an old friend. I had never seen him before, and had expected an older type of person, but he was young and gentle and charming. His warmth and personality engulfed me. The more he spoke, the more impressed I became with his sincerity and love of his people.

I had quite expected to see the King walk through the door, and in a way I was relieved to find that it was his son, Agrippa. This Prince was in the northern part of the land of Egypt, and was placed there by his father to care for that sector of the country – each son of a Herod was given, on reaching a certain age, a part of his father's kingdom to control, or be answerable for. I was in the north – the true palace was far south, more convenient in those times for controlling. For the land of Egypt was mighty and stretched far and wide into what is now called Sudan and other parts.

He asked my help to put over his teachings to the youth of the land. He had heard of me and of my talents. He merely wanted to use me to indoctrinate the young with his religion, which served his aggrandisement. But I was flattered by his attention to me – a mere nobody. He proposed a task for me – a Royal Mission. He asked me to go and think about it.

I went away to think. Wherever I went and mentioned that I had actually spoken with the Prince of Egypt, people of my own class were very suitably impressed. All my old principles had gone by the board – "religion" wasn't so bad now – the Prince couldn't by a lying, cheating, false ruler, using religion for his own ends (as I knew within me). He was sincere and good, and he deserved my total allegiance and service.

In that life I did not resist the temptation of wealth and fame – I sold myself to Religion and the State.

*   *   *   *   *

I relate now to you a happening from the time when I had become well established at the court of the young Herod Agrippa – a happening of horror that it does me no credit to relate – the happening could have been avoided if I had had courage and been truthful in the way of Soul.

It was a vicious time, that of the time of Jesus. Many were injured unnecessarily. The Herod who was the father of my patron had died. He had had many wives, but in particular he had a chief wife, a first-in-line wife, as you may think of her. There was also an older uglier one, but one of influence. The King was to be buried and according to the custom at that particular time, one of the wives was to be buried with him, to "accompany him" on his way to the Land of what we then, in those times, thought was Ra – the so-called place of Gods.

It was the duty of the chief wife to choose the "privileged" one. In this case the young chief wife delegated the choice to the older, ugly one. Now this one had recently been insulted, slighted by a certain other of the young wives, and for revenge she named that one as the one to be buried with her lord.

42

On the day of the burial ceremony, I was wondering if the wife to be buried would know, in advance, who she was who had been chosen. There was much pomp and ceremony that day and, at the crucial moment there were many people all around – standing on terraces. It was in a very religious way – such chantings and priestly splendour – so many sick ones put to death, to appease the so-called gods, in honour of the Herod's journey to Ra. Then after the chantings, the journey started in reality along the river – larger then than now, and cleaner by far, but bloody in effect with the journey.

Too many were killed unnecessarily – too many. What was one more to matter – a young one to be sure, but of such grace and charm.

I start now to put to rights the wrongs of those times. I, Simon could have changed this. I could have taken her as my wife, for I cared, in a way, for her. But to step out in front of all and accept her, at the last moment caused me embarrassment, and I did not wish to look so "wishy-washy" as to want a wife, in those times.

The beautiful lady in silver stooped down, and kissed her two children who were standing with her, said good-bye to them calmly and clearly, stepping down towards an open coffin, in the centre of the scene. I watched as she approached the coffin, and I realised with horror that she had calmly accepted her fate. The shock hit me, and I was revolted. I sold her to their gods by not accepting her as mine.

None had given a thought to the utter despair that was felt by the victim, much less cared. I include myself in that way of being, for although now in Soul I am in a state of caring for all, regardless of self, at that period of my Earth life I had given up the way of Truth for a life of viciousness and love of self.

Many were put to death that day, not only the splendid lady

43

of the courts – but I only tell you of one who related to me personally on that occassion, and so few cared in those times – so few.

*   *   *   *   *

I take you now a few years on in time. It was, in a way, a crucial moment for the success or failure of Jesus.

Jesus had, the previous day, come to see Herod Agrippa in order to tell him of his task in life, to ask him to turn to his Soul, and carry out his part of the Plan – that which he had arranged before he came to Earth. Agrippa was open to be convinced, either way, and in part he was ready to accept the word of Jesus.

Jesus had told him that I too, Simon, had a part in this Great Plan for mankind, but he had not been specific. Agrippa had relayed this to me, saying that it would not require any radical change in my planned way of life.

Now Jesus had been invited to attend again on the second day, and I was present. I was highly sceptical, and really not ready to listen to anything which would upset my present or planned way of life – for I was as you would say "well set-up". I was a materialist, out and out, and I enjoyed and thrived on riches and prestige, and I did not want to give them up in any way – having no intention of doing so.

When Jesus spoke, I realised immediately that what he proposed would drastically affect us – especially me.

Egotism was my driving force in life, prestige my bread and butter, material riches as necessary as the air I breathed. Here was danger! A threat to all I held so dear. Not only did I not wish to listen, but I could not afford Agrippa to be influenced either. So I scoffed. I ridiculed every word that he uttered. I was angry all through the discussion, and I showed it in my derision of Jesus.

But then Jesus turned his attention to me. He explained that "his way", the way of Soul, the way of fulfilling my task in

44

life, by helping to spread the word of Soul, the Absolute, would not really be a radical change in my life – for had I not planned to become a High Priest of the gods of Ra?

It was so that I was planning to become a priest of high rank, but that for me meant further wealth, and pomp and prestige, an even further increment to *my* way of life. Much as in your day Bishops of your land are given the man-title of "Lord", and a prestigious position in your Government of State (House of Lords) and a small "palace", and coloured robes, and have people kneel down to kiss their ring. But this is very pale and drab compared to the pomp and wealth that I would receive, as was the religious fashion in my day.

But this fellow Jesus, he was actually suggesting that I serve the Lord of All Souls *for nothing*, no material reward of any kind, and also that I become a better person – I, friend to the King of all Egypt, Minister of State.

Such was my power and ego and self-esteem, that I did not believe one word of what the Lord Jesus said to Agrippa or myself. I was afraid to even *consider* believing it – because if I did, I might have to give up my Prestige, my cruel power, and also – my nicely increasing wealth. This I placed above the service of any Being. Religion and pomp – yes. But Jesus was asking too much – too much to even consider believing. No wonder I was derisive. I knew that Agrippa was afraid of ridicule more than anything else.

This is how I prevented another Soulpart from doing his task in life, and Jesus from receiving the support that Soul had planned for him before we came to Earth – how I helped the last Soul plan for the salvation of man to come to nought – become just another religion.

It may seem odd to you that, in those far-off times, anyone could be willing to destroy life, just to satisfy some local custom or convention, be it religious or merely social, or both.

I say that a similar thing happens today, in your day and age.

No, not in some far off "primitive land", on some rare occasion of state.

I refer to all of mankind here and now. Every day you are destroying your lives here, with your social and religious customs, sacrificing yourselves and your own Soul even, to the whims of priests and of religious fashion, local social conventions and styles. Yet you do not realise it, because you have never really looked at yourselves with the eye of an outsider – you see all that you do as normal and proper.

Look around you, look at yourselves. From the moment you rise in the morning to the moment you sleep at night, you are following the pagan rituals and self-destructive religious traditions – blindly and unthinkingly.

I will leave you to examine your own typical day in detail, and to sort out those parts of it where you are performing actions merely because you have been told that that is the way things are normally done – and have been done for generations. Or those parts where religion, in one way or another, dictates the way.

Have you the courage to look impartially upon your own way of life – in the same way in which you looked upon the parts of mine which I related to you. I am sure that you looked critically upon the social and religious ways which the fashion of the day dictated, and in which I took part. You looked at them with the eye of one not involved in any way, and you saw the stupidity, futility, cruelty of those ways. Your saw the agony the uncaring of myself and my contempories brought to the victims of custom and religion – and from my vantage point of Soul I agree with you entirely, for I see how all is in reality.

But I am also able to see almost precisely the same features in your society of today. Look with me in my way and you will see that the aims, motives, and methods of religion and those of power have not really changed at all – especially in the

46

aspect of uncaring and cruelty to those who go against the system. Also the careful indoctrination, from baby to adulthood, which leads all to accept as right and proper the viciousness, the ritual and chanting, the dressing up in fancy robes, the judgement of others and – even more so in your day – the wars caused by religion.

All this uncaring, taken to such an extreme degree, causes the leading of such a futile and wasteful way of life – for *none* of man, not one, is fulfilling the task that he set out to do on Earth.

I have paid, and paid dearly, over and over again, for the part I played during my life as Simon – for not only did I not fulfil my purpose on Earth, but I prevented so many, many others from fulfilling their task, too. The extent of my encroachment was vast, but I care enough for you of mankind to try now to help you to evade the ways of folly which I followed so thoroughly.

Examine closely *your* own way of life. Ask yourself why you do each and every thing that you habitually do. Who told you to do it and what were the motives for telling you so? Examine closely the actions and lives of your priests (not just their words) – and remember that I too was once a high priest of such pomp and prestige as would put your bishops and patriarchs to shame. I know how all is with such as they. I too loved to live with the power and riches and life of comfort – with the common masses kneeling before me and kissing the rings on my fingers, or even my feet – as I falsely proclaimed I was an agent of the so-called God of all Gods.

In this manner I helped to dupe so many thousands of people and to destroy so many lives – to turn so many from their true purpose in life.

Priests and perpetrators of religion – I was once as you are, and such now is my care for *all* mankind that I tell you to give up your evil ways – the way of lies – so that you do not have to share the agonies of paying back for all your deeds, which I have been through. I ask you to change before it is too late, for you will not be allowed to fool mankind much longer with your "holy" books and bibles of rubbish.

I begin now to help to put right all the wrongs that I did, and my first task is to show, *to prove*, to all mankind that what is contained in your so-called "holy scriptures" is for the most part completely untrue. Some names you have of those who were around Jesus in those times, many others are sheer invention – almost all of the remainder is merely stories invented hundreds of years later. *I know.*

Yes, I am indeed the Simon of whom you have heard, but I was not, I am so ashamed to admit, any friend or helper of Jesus. All was so utterly different from the way religion tells it.

But *I* do not say idle words and expect all to believe me – as the religious leaders do. No, I come to prove all to you – that is my task. Not when you are dead – but starting now, a few short weeks away.

Listen for me, you who are as I in Soul, and watch for me – for soon I come to guide you on your way. When you meet me you will have no doubts as to who I am – for this time I come with the caring and the strength of Soul.

In other ages, other civilisations, messengers, ambassadors of Soul, have been sent to bring Truth and Understanding to man. Some have been listened to and heeded for a while only, others have been ignored and rejected, and yet others have been persecuted and killed. Such was the case with Jesus.

But this time none of those things will occur. This time we of Soul come in strength, in force of numbers, with a great Power and Intelligence of the Soul of all Souls, the Core of all Power, behind us.

Not only do I say to you that "We come" – I say to you now "We are here!".

CHAPTER FIVE

Now let me tell you of something that has never before been told on this Earth of yours – ever.

Outside of your so-small Earth, of the millions of realms of your Universe, outside of all the Universes in their countless billions, beyond the so-vast expanse of "Space", as described to you, and even beyond the control of the Ultimate, of the Mass of Power, that you may think of as God – there are many other different ways of being, many other so-different beings within their own "areas of substance". So very, very different. We see all around us, and are alert to all – although others are not aware that we observe them. In a way, it is like Man, who does not see his own real Self. We are not though, invisible as such – we have merely taken on a completely different way of being from all others.

The Power that is the Mass controls all that is within our area of substance that is "Space", and will continue to control absolutely for all time to come – there is no other possibility according to the very nature of things. Let this be quite clear.

Allow me to take you in thought to another special area adjoining Our Lands – a place which, in your present bodily state you could not bear to look upon. Rather, I should say, the beings in that area would be too grotesque for your sight to stand. These beings are so, so weird – Man could never imagine just how they are in their unsightliness – even in his hallucinations.

But the fact that they are so different from our formation and way of being, because they are so weird in appearance, does not mean that they are in any way evil. Far from it, for they are Wisdom supreme.

They know of us and at times we have communication with them. More important, we respect each other's ways, the differences of those ways. When we choose to allow them to see us – we to them also seem weird.

They make use of substance in a similar way to us, they put it to use for the benefit of all their kind, and all the beings are in a state of contentment and well-being. They, we understand, were many eons ago in such a state of chaos – as we ourselves had been, but they overcame this with understanding and use of Intelligence – also as we had done.

How they came into being, none knows, not even their Controller, who is such a wondrous being, in understanding, caring, wisdom, and many other ways.

Science fiction places before the minds of Man many differing and gruesome types of being, but he very rarely comes anywhere near to reality, except for tiny snippets, inklings of how things are, which are presented to him by Soul, in order to awaken the torpor of the imagination of Man.

These weird yet wonderful beings adjoin our areas along one part only. They too are constantly on the alert to outside influences, for they are almost surrounded on all other sides, as we are, by areas of beings which differ wildly yet again, from either themselves or from us – beings which are even more weird and outlandish in aspect and way of existence.

It almost seems as if some vast intelligence, gone mad, had tried repeatedly to form something – yet always failing, each time being unsuccessful and leaving the remnants behind to exist independently.

Man strives for understanding of the Unknown, yet little realising that he is in no position to know the truth of all, nor ever will be. Even we do not know – we who can see far and wide over many differing "lands". That is to come.

We, in time and with Soul Power, will extend to the far reaches of the now Unknown. None can prevent us from doing this, such is the nature of the Power that is the Mass, the Energy that is Soul. But do not misunderstand, this does not mean that we will encroach in any way upon those beings who use intelligence for good reasons, for we have no reason to do so, nor is it possible within the Code of Souls, which governs the very existence and way of being of Soul.

But the others, the evil ones – these we soon go forward against, these we will overcome and in the course of time annihilate completely. You may doubt the rightness of such an action, but can anything live in peace and harmony when evil surrounds? Evil is not as we are in any way, nor is it as some others are. Evil, as they are, is persistent, boring, destroying, penetrating – and still it constantly tries to penetrate – Our Lands.

If there remained the slightest chance that the evil ones would change their way – then we would encourage, and finally embrace them and all could join together in peace. But could we not just leave them to their own devices, and keep them out as we do at present? Then realise that those who invade us are all around us constantly, and trying unceasingly in so many ways to penetrate. Would you rather that we remain inactive, and that they destroy us?

In our areas of substance, our Space, we alone exist – and yet they still attempt to pass through, around, or over us – to eventually smother us. In the lands that they now occupy they are bursting at the seams, so over-populated are they with their own beings – and yet they have no intention either of "gathering in" any of their beings, or even of halting their rate of expansion of population. To do so would be completely alien to them, perhaps even impossible to conceive the idea.

In some areas of their lands – or really I should say "volume", for they, like us, live not on a flat plane or surface, but rather as fishes do in a volume of water – in some of these areas, they are as small as pin heads, so continuously do they divide themselves to make more and ever more beings, and disregarding even self as a whole in the doing of it.

Yes, be quite certain they try to overcome without ceasing, tirelessly, relentlessly. They have, even to our knowledge, already taken over at least five other types of areas of substance – *none of the the original beings are left.* They were remorselessly smothered by the greed and evil of these unaccountable beings, who thirst for more, ever more.

In regions beyond these beings there are others who may be likened, in a way, to us – not in form or aspect, for here they are indeed vastly different, but rather in the performance of their way of being, their caring for those which are Self, and their respect for the differences of those other-than-self. They too are alarmed by the very presence and manner of the evil ones, for they are not as we are in resistence and Power of Soul.

Either we can join forces with these ones, and together combat the evil or we can stand aloof and watch so much of good, both Lands and beings, over-ridden by the invaders. There is so much that exists even beyond those areas, but unless we can link with them across the evil ones, we must remain forever virtually isolated within our own area. There is no other alternative, no other way.

These evil ones were the beings that made the Mass – but in doing so ruined themselves. The intelligence which controlled these beings experimented with substance, but had no idea of the extent of the Power with which he played. In the explosion which followed this attempt to force an entry into the area which is now Our Lands, a Mass of Power was projected through, but this brought with it the Intelligence, in some way, from the control of these other beings – or so it would seem. We have no definite proof of this, but in the early ages of the Mass of Power, we viewed the utter ruin of their lands – then suddenly all beings there seemed out of control – and simply multiplied. Now there is none there to contact with any intelligence whatsoever.

In order to behold other areas, you need a way of vision that is no-wise restricted as is the sight of man. We of the Lands of Soul – as we have called them for the benefit of man's understanding – have just such a method of vision.

We have the means and the ability to range far and wide in our viewing, our scanning of other lands. Not with eyes, such as man has, but with the Power and Intelligence of Soul. It may seem odd to your way of looking at it – but it is, nevertheless, a fact. You may consider it as a huge lens, circling the Power that is the Mass. We see all that is in the line of vision, and we would be able to see much more, were it not for the fact that, in part, our sight is blocked by the evil ones. And by these we are near to being surrounded, cut off from all else that is – though not quite so. Only the strength of those others who are such as we, has left open the channel of communication. These we must support.

But now we come to the crux of the whole matter – what can man do about any of this? I will tell you, and this part is vital to your own very existence as mankind.

Now we make arrangements to go forward over the areas of evil which surround us – but before we can do so, *man must conform to the way of Soul.*

Out of all the Universes in the Lands of Soul, man is the only section that is indolent of Soul, that is not earning, making Power for Soul. This means that in order to start to go forward we must either rid ourselves of man, "fold him in", or give him his last chance to "turn on" the Power for Soul, to release the essential energy that Soul requires.

Time for mankind to know Truth. Now you must be told, for the first time ever, how things really are. We comouflage, *we use the system of the Earth within each Universe as a means of fulfilling the Power in a Soul.*

It is not necessary to the well-being of Soul, that man be allowed to continue as he is. It is only essential to Soul that, if mankind is allowed to continue to exist, he must earn for self and for Soul, by creating the necessary Energy for his Soul.

Soul, at a mere glance could put man away from him, withdraw his existence, but we always try to retain all the beings that belong to, and form a part of our Great Soul . . . *as long as the well-being of the whole of Soul is in no way endangered by their continued existence.*

We adore all beings that are Soul. We respect and care for all to the highest degree. That is the Code of Souls. To despise has never been our way, but the way which man likes, and follows, leads him in the end to the state of being despised by all others – even his own Soul.

It has been arranged by Soul that the Earth of each Universe serves two purposes. One, it is used as a means of Soulparts gaining experiences and evolving, by earning, and secondly, it is used as a means of creating Power for the Soul of that Universe, until the Universe becomes "fulfilled" and has sufficient impetus to create Power *of itself.*

All Souls radiate from the Ultimate in a net-work of branches, so that each one is linked through its own "line", to the Ultimate. Each fulfilled, Energy-producing Soul (or Universe), then sends the excess Power produced along its line to the Ultimate.

From there, the Power is "processed" at the Core of the Mass, a certain Essence added to it, and then it is distributed as required for the benefit and well-being of all.

Evolved Soulparts come forward along the link of Universes, and are made into Souls, and given the Power to begin their own Universe. As new Universes are created, and as fulfilled Universes grow and expand in Power and Intelligence within the Mass of Power, so the Mass itself expands, until the

Universes of the Lands of Soul fill all of Space to the very boundaries, making all secure.

Then we will be in a position to go forward and extend ourselves, to be free for ever from the evil ones, free to link with the lands beyond.

You cannot realise the extent of the blockage of the flow of Power to the Ultimate that this Earth of yours is causing. Know then that there are a great number of Universes created after this one, and linked to it in line. The Power from all of them must flow through this Universe of yours in order to reach the Ultimate, and the amount of Universes affected by your blockage is roughly *One Million*.

That is the extent of the blockage that you are causing, the extent of the harm that you are doing to the Mass of Power, to Soul, to Self. So many Soulparts are being held up from progressing to the state of Soul. So much energy is being wasted by this Universe, that should be benefitting the Soul.

You, man, are as a parasite feeding on the Mass, and contributing nothing, earning nothing. That is how Soul sees you. Unless constantly fed with Power from the other Universes this one would disintegrate to nothingness.

Even your Earth has slowed down so much that, in time as man reckons, comparing with the other Universes, one hundred years are as one year on Earth. So slow, so slow.

Until the blockage is cleared it would be futile to keep adding more Universes to the lineage, for it would only add to the burden of Soul.

There are so many fulfilled Universes that the Ultimate is able to keep on "pulsing" constantly – receiving Power, processing, and distributing – but to be minus the Power of so many Universes (whilst having expanded to contain them) must put a strain on all the others.

This is why even the animals, birds, and insects on the Earth now all take part to try to rectify the situation. They are earning for Soul, whereas man is not. In general, they listen to their Soul, they follow the way directed by their Soul, and in doing so they earn by producing Energy for the Soul of this Earth. (Now you have the explanation for what you call "instinct").

Soul has arranged the nature of things within Soul so that all must flow continuously. We are not able to sustain all, unless all Universes, all Souls, play their part. That is why it is so important for the good of all, that all evolve, and that nothing is given without the earning, ever.

That is why the useless line of one million Universes is as a dead weight to Soul, as a withered arm is to a man. It is like a cancer eating away his insides – for all is within the Mass of Power.

Do you now realise, man, what you are the cause of? Do you see clearly what could result from your indolence, your laziness in following the Soul way? Can you now understand the urgency of the situation?

Think deeply of what I have told you of the evil ones, the invaders, they that would smother us into extinction. The Earth of man could destroy the whole of these Lands of Ours – not just the Earth, but all of the Universes of the Lands of Soul – if we allowed man to carry on in the way he is now.

But he will not be allowed to do so. This is man's last chance. There is no question of what the decision will be if we have to choose to sacrifice man of this Earth, or jeopardise the Lands of Soul and all in them.

Nostradamus warned mankind for he knew without doubt what was to be – but was scoffed at. In time he closed himself away from the jeers of society and even of his own family.

He was no scientist, but thought himself one. At times he took on self-grandeur to cover up his failings of fear.

His warnings are about to come true if man does not change, although his words have been distorted and "interpreted", as have been the words of many others. Many others have also, from time to time, warned man of the dire need to change, and of the consequences for ignoring – but mostly these thoughts, too, have been distorted, coloured and interpreted in the way of the fashionable religion of the day, in that particular area of land.

I must finally remind you once more of the advent of the evil ones, the invaders from beyond the Lands of Soul – of how the one single being of them penetrated unknown and undetected into one of the Mighty Universes – how it proliferated, by dividing itself constantly and repeatedly, on such a grand scale. How the invasion of the beings was finally detected, and how the Might of the Power of Souls struck down these beings from elsewhere. But how, first of all, the Universe in its entirety had to be folded in, disintegrated, as being the only way in which the beings could be destroyed also.

The Soulparts of that unfortunate Universe agreed willingly to be withdrawn so as to provide a way, the only way of saving all the other Universes of Our Lands. I say "unfortunate" Universe only in one sense, for soon the Wonderful Soul of that Universe, given special aid from the Ultimate of Souls, will cause to blossom forth again in even greater glory, a new Universe more Mighty that the first – and honoured by all of Soul for the sacrifice it willingly made for the good of all.

Those of this Earth Plane, the Soulparts, think only of the good and benefit of Self, although their Soul is truly Wondrous and would give all for others. But have no doubts that we would have no hesitation in crushing this Earth to dust, in a flash, if this became necessary *in order to save all others* of the Lands of Soul. That situation is almost upon us.

Your own Soul says so.

Whether it becomes necessary or not, rests entirely with you.

CHAPTER SIX

There are among you, men and women of the medical profession, experts in matters of the brain, or of the mind. But just how far have they reached in solving the mysteries of thought, of memory, of activating the body – of intelligence?

They have not even dented the surface in the probing of even one of these aspects of the mind.

I listen to your experts of the brain, and I hear only long and complex ramblings in the special language or jargon of the profession – which mean absolutely nothing. Not any single one of them can tell you even what a thought is, let alone where or how a thought is made.

Now is the time to look afresh at aspects of life on this Earth of yours, and the most important aspect of all is the one about which man knows absolutely nothing – the aspect of thought. And how can he, when all his basic assumptions about the mind of man are competely wrong?

For countless centuries, through differing civilisations, man has been exploring many avenues to try to puzzle out the 'mystery' of the mind. Yet never has he done so despite all his efforts, for always he has been looking in the wrong direction. And what is more, the experts of the day *have always been followers* in almost every way – following the ideas of others who themselves did not understand what they talked about.

Those of you who consider yourselves to be scientists and researchers now – you too are merely followers, in spite of the fact that you may have an idea or two which you regard as original. You have not been able to help being so, for in your schools, colleges, and universities, you had your grounding, learned your basic principles and were indoctrinated with a way of thinking – and all this was *based on wrong assumptions of others who had failed* to discover what you seek. All the books that you were forced to read were written by those who did not even know what a thought is. And you were *made to follow them*.

A leader in the field you may even consider yourself to be now – but you were set on a certain road, a certain way of struggling for understanding, by your predecessors. You had no alternative. You had no other way to turn to but the logic of man in your given method of searching, for your teachers knew no other way.

But logic needs absolute truths upon which to base its reasoning – and your predecessors had none, just as you have none. You, who would be leaders, through no fault of your own are followers – no matter how high in your profession you rank.

But now we have arrived at the dawn of the Golden Age of Understanding. Now is the time when the so-called "mysteries of life" are to be unfolded to man, if he cares to listen to them. And the wonders of this age will be revealed to man through those few who have the courage to have and to use an *open mind,* those few who have the courage to allow themselves to become inspired by the Intelligence of the Universe.

The Soul of this Universe, who is its Power and Intelligence, now looks for men of calibre, men not afraid to look in a new direction, where Truth and Discovery lie – men who will not hold back because they fear the ridicule of their envious fellows.

Soul looks for *Leaders of Men*.

If you are such a man of science, turn now from your blind alleys and the fumblings which you have been led into. Break out of your straight jacket of thought and set your sights on using the genius that Soul will send *to you*.

Mankind is in need of leaders to bring him out of the uncertainty and aimlessness which plagues his very life – because of his unknowing or non-understanding. Mankind will be forever in the debt of those first to venture into the unknown and to make that unknown as clear and simple for them as a daisy in a sunlit field. I speak to those who have the facilities and ability not yet available to the mass of mankind. I will point the way to look, and the Supreme Intelligence of this Universe, your own Soul, will inspire you with the sight of genius, the secrets of life itself will become your oyster.

There are only two requirements to be a Leader of Mankind in discovery – one is that you have the *courage to have an open mind,* the other is that you be *among the first.*

Real man of science, step forward now with those of us of the Lands of Soul – and you will inherit the Earth. Or stand back and be a follower.

Mankind awaits you! Will *you* fail him?

I begin to tell you of other items that should be of interest to you.

The way of the body is so interesting, once you have a clear understanding of how it truly works – but it can appear so complex and mystifying to one who looks in the wrong way. I can enlighten you concerning the main workings of the body and mind, if you will read what I say with an attitude of listening rather than of criticising before you consider.

A motor car or similar machine will normally keep running as long as the necessary fuel is fed into it, but to get it to start going in the first place it needs some form of impetus, such as a spark, to set it off.

The body is just the same. Relax in mind whilst I explain.

The body of a baby within the host mother, resides encased in a sac which is filled with fluid, and linked to the mother by means of a tube. *This tube allows the child free movement, and in no way does it feed the child whilst it is in this sac of liquid.*

The "water" is quite necessary for the tiny body to allow it to move about freely, so as to avoid cramping or damaging the limbs by pressure too long in one spot.

At this stage of its existence the body within the walls of the womb is *not* a living being. In no way is it alive, for it is merely a piece of growing and forming substance. It cannot think or see or hear or feel. It has a brain forming it is true, but it has not the *impetus* which gives it life. This it receives *after* being ejected from the womb of the mother.

Up to this point the being, the Soulpart which planned to enter and use that body, can change its mind about reliving on Earth, if it so wishes. There are so many abortions or still-births.

First the fluid surrounding the body is released and this forces open and lubricates the channel through which the baby will pass. A short time later the baby is ejected also. As soon as it comes out into the world it gives a gasp, an intake of breath – its very first breath, and at that moment its life has begun, and it begins to cry. At that moment the being that is the impetus has entered the body, and from that point it no longer has the option to withdraw.

The key to the life of a being on Earth is a triangle. To understand the workings of that triangle is to understand the meaning of "life", of the body and mind of man. The first and most important point of the triangle of life is a part of the body to which man gives little attention – the Pancreas.

I have explained to you about the two tracks of thought which operate the body functions and actions – the Original track, which is used for all conscious thoughts and actions, from which you make your decisions in selecting the right or wrong way to go – and the Secondary or Duplicate track, which operates directly, of its own accord, all the workings of all the organs of the body. Now it might make it clearer to understand if you regard two tracks of thought as two sides of a tape of a computer which have been recorded before hand, with a sort of pre-arranged pattern or programme.

At the moment of the first breath or intake of air, the impetus takes it upon itself to set the tracks in the right place in the Pancreas. The Duplicate track then takes over the normal running of the Body, the lungs begin to breath in air, the baby cries and its life on Earth has begun.

During the period from conception to the birth, the Soulpart has the chance to cancel its planned life on Earth, to choose to postpone it to a later time. Even in that decision, the Soulpart always has been given free choice. You must realise that it takes great courage for a Soulpart to decide to come to this Earth as it is now.

A Soulpart, with the help and guidance of Soul, plans the sort of life that it is going to have, long before it arrives on Earth. Each time it comes to Earth, it intends to fulfil its task of earning Power for its Soul, and it sees that that is difficult enough in these ages of indoctrination and encroachment by others. Then there is the diversion from its task which it will have to face and which it will be taught by Society and Religion whilst it is still young in body and defenceless in mind. Also, it arranges for itself ways in which it will pay back for harm done to others in past lives. This it wishes to do, for it knows that it cannot begin to evolve until it has paid for every wrong action ever committed. Each being judges itself – no other judges – and each being arranges in advance how it will repay.

If it has in the past deprived others of food or drink, it might arrange to be born in a famine or drought-stricken area. If it has ill-treated those of another race, it may arrange to be born of that race, and so suffer similar persecution. All is easy for Soul to arrange.

You can see therefore, that it would require much courage under those circumstances to leave a state of peace of mind and enjoyment to place yourself on this devastated Earth, controlled by those indoctrinators of religion and the ways of society, who would force their way on to your body and mind from the moment that you arrive.

Up to the point of birth, the Soulpart has free choice to withdraw, but once the impetus is planted in the Pancreas and the birth completed there is no turning back. How is it that man in his waywardness has managed to reverse all things from the way that they should be, were intended to be? He now celebrates and rejoices when a new-comer is born to this place of uncaring and suffering, of cruelty and destruction. Yet he wails and complains when a Soulpart "dies" and passes on to a high state of existence unimaginable to man.

Once the impetus is placed into the Pancreas at birth, that baby can be regarded as a "being" for the first time. From that moment it is no longer just a piece of flesh and bone attached to and supported by the host-mother – it is a being in its own right.

The tape or tracks of thought then take over the job of running the body. The Secondary track of thought directs the operation of all the organs and parts of the body which do not need a deliberate action on the part of the being. All these operations are quite automatic – the breathing, pumping of blood, healing of wounds, growing of hair, and so on. The Secondary track sends out sensing thought impulses to all sections of the body, and receives constant reports of their condition and functioning. It then carries out any adjustments or alterations necessary according to the thought pattern on the track. A Soulpart may have decided in order to pay back for wrongs in a previous life or lives, to be born blind or deaf or dumb, or with some other disability. All this is already accounted for within the pattern of the secondary thought track, and such differences are arranged directly from the Pancreas to the organs concerned. *It is natural.*

63

Apart from this, the instructions from the Pancreas will go on operating the body in a perfectly normal way – unless the body is interfered with by medical men and such like, or the being himself. Irreparable damage may be performed by interfering with the body, but one thing that can never be altered by another is the moment of death. The precise second when a Soulpart returns home to Soul is arranged accurately and *is never changed* by another being or by Soul, in any circumstances.

It is so important to understand this point clearly. You may be the most reckless car driver or mountain climber on Earth, and you may break every bone in your body, as well as lose all your senses – but you will not die one split second before your appointed, pre-planned time has arrived for you to return home. Know it to be so.

The difference between life or death in the physical body of a being on Earth is merely the presence of the Impetus. The lump of flesh and blood, etc., that is the beginnings of a baby in the womb of the mother, is lifeless. It just has no life of its own. It does not become a living being until a certain Impetus is placed in it by Soul. In fact, this Impetus, this thing which sets off and maintains life in the body – *it is the being itself*. The Impetus is the Soulpart occupying the cocoon, the body.

The Soulpart does not begin its existence upon Earth until it is implanted in the selected body of the "baby" at the exact moment of birth. You yourself are *not* a body containing some sort of life force – you *are* the life force occupying a body, which you entered at "birth" and will discard at the "death".

You enter the body in the form of thought. You speak, eat, sleep, love, hate and so on, all by means of thought. You *are* in the form of thought.

Now, when the Impetus is implanted in the body, it brings with it two patterns or tracks of thought, rather like programmes fed into a computer. One track deals with the *functioning of the body* – its health, size, shape, etc. – and the other with the *way a person 'thinks'*.

Now it is important to realise that thought is not some airy-fairy notion, an abstract idea – thought is real substance and it must exist in a "place", just as all other substances must, even though it is not touchable or measurable by man. Because of this, the Impetus and that which contains the thought patterns must reside in some place in the body in order to be able to operate, to enable the Soulpart to function as a being. *That location is the Pancreas.*

We have discussed the pattern of thought placed inside the Pancreas which gives instructions by means of thought impulses, to all the organs of the body, and so keeps all working as planned – depending on how the thought pattern was arranged before the Soulpart came to Earth. I have compared it with one track on a computer tape which is a "programme" capable of working out all the actions necessary to be taken to keep a body working normally, and capable of setting all the working parts of the body in motion. For convenience, I call this the Secondary or Duplicate track of thought.

Now we come to that arrangement of thoughts which is the source of all conscious and deliberate actions – the Original track of thought. You could think of it as being on the other side of the tape placed in the Pancreas. Again this is a pattern of thought which allows for all the possible thoughts and actions which the being can use, but it operates in a completely different way from the Duplicate track.

There is a stream or channel of fluid which links the Pancreas to the Brain, and as long as the Soulpart remains within the body, that flow of fluid remains unbroken even for a fraction of a second. The Original track of thoughts is constantly sending a stream of thought to the brain along that channel.

The brain is only a receiving set, and *not* a thinking machine as man of this age has been led to believe. No brain has ever produced one single thought, and never will. All thoughts which activate the brain come to it via the link to the Pancreas and the Impetus, the thought track stored there.

The brain is part of the physical cocoon and one day dies. The Impetus is the being that is you – and never dies.

Placed just below the underside of the brain there is a Selector. This Selector is constantly scanning all aspects of the brain – to and fro, to and fro – millions of times a minute. It receives, sorts, and selects thoughts from the Original track, and applies them to those areas of the brain concerned with implementing them. These are all conscious thoughts, along the Original track, although two types of thought are sent for use or rejection. "Right" thoughts and "wrong" thoughts.

Now by "right" thoughts I mean those which are in accordance with your pre-arranged plan in life, the ones which will cause you to fulfil your life's task, your destiny as man. By "wrong" thoughts I mean those alternative thoughts which are sent in accordance with what you *want* or *like* to do – in order that you may always have free choice – an essential factor of your life as man. All your actions such as speaking, running, looking, and so on, are of this nature, and are triggered off through the brain. These thoughts can over-ride bodily functions triggered off by thought impulses from the Duplicate track. For example, your breathing may be slow and gentle because you are relaxed and calm, but you can, by means of choosing to put to use an Original or deliberate thought, change that motion of the lungs to a quick and harsh way of breathing. The thought from the Original track over-rode the thoughts of the Duplicate.

Although the function of the Duplicate track is to keep the body functioning normally, it may have been planned by the Soulpart to have a deformed limb, such as a "withered arm". The Duplicate pattern is set therefore to restrict the supply of necessary substances to the arm which enable it to grow normally. On the other hand, a person may have a perfectly normal arm which suddenly becomes "paralysed". This non-movement of the arm is brought about through no impulses being sent from the sector of the brain dealing with arm movements. This is usually caused through no thoughts being sent along the Original track to the brain. Such occurrences are often necessary to change the life pattern of a Soulpart who deviates too far from his pre-planned life pattern. This is usually the case with many illnesses and body malfunctions, such as Ulcers or Arthritis. In most cases, if the person would only stop what he was doing (in occupation, way of playing, way of treating another, etc.), then the illness would disappear.

It is so important to realise that *the cause* of any illness or malfunction of an organ *is never within a body.*

The cause is always to be located in the way a person uses his thoughts – except for certain happenings which were planned as a repayment from an earlier life. And even many of those can be avoided by the correct use of thought. *It is natural.*

There is one exception to the principle that bodily malfunctioning can be put right by changing to the correct use of thought. When the receiving set which is the brain, by means of which the Original thought track controls the body, is interfered with by medical men, experimenters, and such like, it is often damaged beyond repair. This is commonly done by means of surgery, giving drugs, or blindly pouring massive doses of electrical current into the brain. In each of these cases, millions of units of the brain are destroyed permanently, and all hope of bodily or mental function in a mormal way destroyed with them.

Certain ones of man do untold harm to the health and sanity of many – by playing with the minds of others whilst being in a state of total ignorance themselves. *Never* do they do any lasting good to their victims.

It has never been understood by man of this civilisation (and I include the last few thousand years) that the body is a pro-duce-producing machine, that the body itself is sustained and operated by means of thought and many organs are geared to cleansing any intake, and processing and concentrating into Output.

The lungs are as bellows whose main purpose is to operate the pump which you call the heart. The blood flows around the body picking up the dross and impurities from various parts. It flows through the pump and on to the Liver. The Liver cleanses the blood and passes the impurities out directly through the Urine in a way of concentrated produce.

The purified blood then passes on to the bone structure where there are countless tiny veins, which feed the bone with what is acquired through the Liver.

The Pancreas itself is also a cleansing agent, as it sorts out the rubbish from both the Stomach and the Kidneys.

When all that is required by the cocoon has been extracted and passed along, then the organs get down to the task of concentrating all that remains into a form ready to be Output – in the form of Urine and Excretia. In fact, all the Output of the body of man is really merely concentrated vegetation, which in turn is merely a form of Soil. All the vegetation that ever grows on Earth is just processed Soil – even the dead bodies which many of you eat are formed from processed vegetation – which is formed from processed Soil.

So you see that the Output of man is concentrated Soil which, if placed directly into the ground and covered im-mediately, would quickly mingle with the other Soil, and so replace all the goodness which had been extracted from it previously.

The Stomach has the capacity of breaking down all forms of vegetation taken into it, of dealing with all minute forms of life within it – except for the bodies of other beings and foods made from such. The body was not designed to deal with parasites from the bodies of other beings (animals, birds and insects), and so has no way of dealing with them.

Most of the painful and deadly deseases of the carnivorous sections of the population are caused by such eating habits. They are not just a punishment for "eating your brothers" – that follows later – they are just the natural, unavoidable consequence of mis-using the cocoon you inhabit.

Now perhaps you can see what constitutes the Triangle of Life of the body of man. The three points are the Mouth, which is the inlet – the Pancreas, which is the Motor providing the power for all the organs to work – and the Anus, which is the outlet for the finished product of the machine that is the body.

When processed further by the Earth itself, the substance that was inactive Soil is on the way to becoming the active Power that will charge the Universe – and earn for the Soul-parts of Earth a state of existence far beyond man's wildest dreams.

Each of man has planned a certain thought pattern with his Soul – one which will enable him to do very well indeed, with maximum ease and efficiency, the task he came to do in life, if he chooses the right way to go. How futile and cruel therefore, to force a child or adult to "learn" the way of another, what another sees fit.

For one who is destined to be one of the most important producing members of society, say a fruit or vegetable farmer, to be forced to learn rules of grammar of a language, or of wars and killings of by-gone times, or of the mathematics of algebra – this is sheer stupidity and cruelty. It is tearing away a being from his purpose in life for the convenience of someone else, who wishes to impose what *he* sees fit onto all others. Do not those who acquire wealth through the operation of large factories need "factory fodder" – rows upon rows of hundreds of thousands of beings all trained or "educated" to be useful members of society – merely because "they" think it should be that way.

Let me make it clear now, so that no one has the excuse of saying that he did not know or understand – all of those who indulge in the mass indoctrination of young ones by force are deliberately depriving those beings of fulfilling their purpose in life, by imposing upon them in a cruel way (mental and physical) the stupid ways arranged by others, who are totally ignorant of the purpose in life of any individual.

I state, merely as a fact of Truth, and not as a criticism or threat in any way – that all who plan and all who carry out such methods of forcibly imposing indoctrinaton upon the young and defenceless in schools or similar ways – they pay, and pay dearly. It is the law of the Universe, the Code of Soul.

It is a fact that *most* young ones in schools go through agony of mind daily through being compelled to go hour upon hour being forcibly fed with what, for them, is useless rubbish, mostly of mis-information.

To a teacher or officer of education it may seem easy, as well as desirable, to learn to read and write or calculate or memorise supposed facts – but to another it may be sheer agony. It all depends upon that one's purpose in life and his prearranged thought pattern. Soul arranges to include in the thought pattern of each *all the knowledge and understanding necessary to carry out the set task in life.*

Cruelty also lies in the overwhelming pressures put upon the prisoner-pupil from all sides – teachers, parents, society all round. He is constantly fed with the idea that to train to obtain and do a "job" as society deems suitable is the be-all and end-all of life. All else is failure and brings punishment in one form or another. This system produces all sorts of nervous and physical illnesses, disorders of the mind, all sorts of violent

70

traits in the systematically twisted minds of the victims of indoctrination.

Nearly all of man on this Earth never have a chance to use in a good way the pattern which they arranged before they came, a chance to excel in their own field, to do in an easy and comfortable manner the task they came to do, for the benefit of mankind. Instead they are forced into always choosing the wrong way to go, the wrong track of thought, in an effort to conform with what others *say* is best for them.

Would you knowingly wish to be the cause of one, six, hundreds or even thousands of Soulparts being taken from their true purpose in life, being taken from the way of listening to the wisdom of their own Soul, of using the right thought track? If you only knew of the penalty of such a thing, without any possibility of escape, then I am sure that *you* would choose the right track of thought in this matter. You would then be giving yourself a chance to begin to fulfil your own destiny, to overcome your own years of indoctrination. Life would then become so easy for you, for all the Intelligence necessary for a full and useful life, a life of enjoyment of everything that you do, is just waiting for you – untapped, unused in any way.

Your own form of genius awaits you, free – but you will not find it in any book, even this one – for my purpose is to guide you to the wisdom of *your* own Soul.

CHAPTER SEVEN

Civilisations. Ancient civilisations. "Lost" civilisations. How they excite the imagination of man! How much he talks about them, debates them, writes countless books about them, and tells stories about them. Man loves civilisations of the past. And yet he has knowledge of only one – the present civilisation.

All the other brief periods of history which he classes as civilisations, such as those of the Incas and Aztecs, the Greeks and the Turks, the Romans and the Chinese, and so on – all of these periods are but small fragments of the one civilization. For man is now at the tail-end of a civilisation which stretches back beyond all historical memory, and man is at one of his most primitive stages in the slide towards complete degeneracy of way of being and crudity of technology.

The true civilisations which I speak of are those which lasted tens of thousands, even hundreds of thousands of years, stretching back over the last say, five million years.

The duration of the first one was around one million years. All other civilisations of the past have been far more developed in the way of knowledge, travel, mental powers, and achievements than the abysmal one that you belong to today. And each one has been ended by means of upheavals in the surface of the Earth – caused always through man's action in neglect of his Earth – upheavals causing lands to sink beneath oceans, mountains to be formed, and lands to rise out of the waters, causing millions of Soulparts to return home to the Transit Realms, and leaving but a few chosen ones to survive. These served to be used as a basis on which to build a new, differing civilisation.

Some have been, in part, on the lands which exist and are used today, others where mighty oceans now roar, others where ice-caps now freeze the life out of the land.

But why? Why should this be? – If some of the civilisations were far more advanced than this one, why the need to start all over again – to start from scratch as it were?

The reason is simple! The beings that were man, that were on Earth at those times were not fulfilling their purpose in life, their Soul reason for being there at all. They had stopped fulfilling the purpose of their existence, and they stubbornly refused to do so, point blank, even though time after time messengers had been sent from the Lands of Soul, to remind them what their purpose was, and to warn them of the only possible consequence of such a life of futility. Annihilation!

Each civilisation started off afresh, and even at times a messenger was listened to and heeded, for a period of time. But always, subsequently, the same dismal pattern was repeated – of man choosing, with eyes open, not to fulfil the purpose of his existence to evolve by earning Power for the Soul of this Universe, but rather to go his own way, to follow his own emotions and to place his own Universe, as well as his own existence, in jeopardy, by leading a life of non-earning – a life of futility and waste.

Always, all during the past five million years, ever since man's inception upon this planet, has he been free to go the way he deemed to be best. Man has free choice.

You have already been told several times that you have free choice – free to choose the way of Soul, your natural way, or the way that leads to annihilation. But do you really understand what that means, how I mean it?

Your leaders and experts in the fields of philosophy and religion and psychology repeatedly tell you that you have "free will". But have you? And what do they mean by it? They state that they mean that you have the freedom to choose from an infinite variety of ways, or at least all the ways that are possible. And you, without really considering, and because you have not understood the ways or origin of thought, have blindly believed this.

I say that free will, as you know it, does not exist. Let me explain exactly what I mean by this, and how the fallacy of so-called "free will" comes about.

When the beings that were man were first placed upon the Earth, they received from their Soul *pure thought* – thought uncontaminated and undistorted in any way by emotions, wrong thought, or any of the ways common to man today. Man received pure thought of Soul and used this thought to capacity, implementing each thought in the correct manner. He enjoyed all things and he lived a full and harmonius life – *and he lived it to capacity*. Man received from his all-caring Soul, and in using what he received, he earned Power for his Soul, for his Universe. At the same time man evolved on his own account, and needed but one enjoyment-crammed, swiftly-passing life on Earth to fulfil his task and pass on to enjoy the bliss of the evolved realms of his Universe.

During the whole of the first era of man on his Earth all went so well. Only thoughts of value, as Soul required, were sent to him. Then he became indolent in the use of these thoughts. At that time he received no thoughts of wrong-doing, and no thoughts of, say, harming another being. Later, Soul provided alternative thoughts to those of value – thoughts of lesser value were intermingled with them, to give man the opportunity of overcoming his changed conditions.

Now man controls his own choice of the use of what Soul sends; but *Soul controls what is sent to choose from – Soul controls the situations – in full*.

Soul arranges all to suit his way – at present, or up to the present, the way of giving to man what he wants, more and more of rubbish. Man chooses, true. But it is Soul who arranges what are the alternatives given to man to choose between. All situations are controlled and arranged by Soul. It is futile of man to plan and scheme – to anticipate, to try to allow for all continguencies. Only Soul knows what all the possible contingencies may be. Many contingencies or possible happenings or situations just do not occur to man in thought – because Soul, the origin of those thoughts, simply does not send any idea, any inkling, of most of the ways it is possible to go.

And man imagines that he controls!

When the indolence crept in and man gradually began to neglect to use *all* that he received – some of the ways of value of Soul were lost. Some of these ways did not affect the fulfilment of man's primary purpose on Earth, but there came a time when this did occur. At that stage man neglected to perform that simple task that would earn Power for his Soul – he neglected to put his Output into the soil and cover it. The rot had set in – the beginning of the end of the first civilisation.

Man had exercised for the first time the power of free choice – of whether to use the pure thoughts, the thoughts of value or not to use them.

At that point a contingency plan was put into operation by Soul, and millions of Soulparts were brought home. A few survivors were left to build again a civilisation geared to the Powering of the Universe and the evolution of the beings of Earth.

Each civilisation has its own thought pattern, and the countless billions of thoughts for each and every individual were all within the confines of the set pattern of thought for that particular civilisation.

If it were possible for a man to look back upon the way of being of another civilisation, it would be completely incomprehensible to him. All that he witnessed would appear both bewildering and illogical, or else fantastic and magical – but in any case un-understandable.

A good example of this, in a way, is man's present non-understanding of animals and their way of being. Man looks at Dolphins, sees that there appears to be some sort of affinity with them, sees how the Dolphin many times helps man with apparent understanding of man's needs. So he studies the Dolphin, teaches him "tricks", records and tries to analyse his language. But because the animal does not under any circumstances take on the way of man, does not seem to "think" in the same way, man eventually comes to the conclusion that the Dolphin is a little intelligent, but far behind man in this respect – when in fact the intelligence of a Dolphin is *far higher* than that of man at present. It is just that the two species of being have a quite different thought pattern, and by the very nature of thought, one cannot possibly understand a type of thought (and the subsequent actions) that one has not experienced directly oneself. It remains forever an alien and inexplicable concept.

But it is not possible to look back upon another civilisation, for Soul has obliterated it all but a few tantalising signs of what once was – as with the Pyramids. This is so that man does not observe other ways of being which he does not comprehend, which are outside of his own thought pattern. The memory is wiped away, just as the memory of how man is in Soul is wiped away.

Man is given a certain thought pattern to think with so that he may choose, in a very limited way, to follow the natural way of Soul or experimentally go down the long tunnel of the way of lesser value put to him. He has a chance to overcome, but the limitations of a thought pattern are set to make that choice simple and clear, to limit the number and complexity of obstacles which he can place there for himself.

It is rather like giving a young child a packet of cigarettes or cigars to smoke, to allow him to refuse the offer, or to smoke them and become sickened by them, and so to understand the folly of that way of drugs.

But in the case of man – of each other civilisation as well as that of today – he grasps for and smokes all of the cigarettes and craves more and more and more – never being satisfied but wanting forever stronger and fouler drugs.

The drugs of the present civilisation are the indoctrinations and rituals of religion and traditions of society.

Man always reverses all that Soul sends – uses all in the opposite way.

In this particular civilisation Soul has eased the burden on man by giving a thought pattern which allows much more leeway, one which makes it easier to choose the Soul way, the thoughts of value, and leaves it harder to choose the ugly thoughts which lead man down the tunnel of ignorance, superstition, brutality, viciousness. But still man has managed to choose the latter.

Soul has eased the burden on man in this age, has given man an easier task with less to overcome, for one reason – that this is the last civilisation to be free to choose evil and reject Soul. In the same way that the ways of being of earlier civilisations (other thought patterns) have been annihilated, so will this way of being also be annihilated – and with it mankind as he is today – unless he turns to Soul now.

Unless he makes this last, final choice in the right way – *listens to and follows the thoughts of value* of his own Soul – then that dark tunnel where man is deeply headed at this moment, will terminate soon and suddenly in eternal blackness.

The way of being of man of this final age will disappear. The beings that are man today will disappear. The individuals that are the Soulparts that have failed to fulfil their task on Earth will cease to be.

The choice is yours, *now* — eternal continuity or annihilation. The Truth is always simple.

Free choice has constantly been given to man, in order that he may have chance after chance to evolve. Man has constantly free choice to take the right way, the *natural way*, or the wrong way – up to a certain point in time.

That point in time has now been reached. Soul has tolerated the waywardness of man right up to the point where, because of the chosen way of man, the very Universe itself is in peril. But now the point has been reached, and man is free to make the final choice, *the ultimate choice – the Soul way or annihilation*.

Man is now about to be obliged to make his final, irrevocable decision – from which there is no turning back. Either he turns to the way of making Power for his Soul, or the total way of being of man is to be brought to extinction – as the light of a candle is snuffed out.

Now it is necessary to be absolutely clear on what is meant by "annihilation". Nothing within all the Universes of Soul can be totally destroyed – for although substance may cease to exist in one form, it cannot do so without changing to exist in a different form. All in all Universes is substance. Soul is substance. Soulparts are substance.

In the case of this Universe of man being folded in, the particles of substance, which are the Soulparts called man, would merely be drawn into their Soul once again, from where they originated. That part of Soul which was a billion Soulparts will *not* cease to be in existence – that is not possible. But the "individuality" that each Soulpart is conscious of being whilst on Earth, that would have been completely annihilated from its own Soul and made ready to link with another Soul – The Wise One.

Now the Universe of the Wise One, as has been relayed through the pen of one other than my scribe, is a Universe which houses the Soulparts from any Universe, which failed to fulfil their task upon their Earth, which refused to evolve in any way in spite of countless opportunities given by their own Soul.

It is there that they must pay for all harm they have ever done – but in conditions completely devoid of any scrap of comfort in any way. Such Soulparts are completely severed from their own mother Soul and never returned. They become linked with the Soul that is the Wise One in the cold, hard Universe of the misfits. In such conditions the dregs of all the Universes are given no freedom, no choice but to comply in full with the now agonising process of evolution – the slow and hard way.

Such is meant by the annihilation of a Soulpart.

At the very beginning of your own Universe the Soul took a part of Self and divided it up to form billions of Soulparts – each with a certain individual life of its own, each with the chance and the potentiality of evolving and becoming eventually a Soul in its own right.

You, as you are now, as you are conscious of being, would cease to exist.

Nothing of itself is ever destroyed by Soul, but now the point in time is reached when man faces real extinction of being, as he knows it. So choose, you of mankind, for the very last time. Soul has been waiting. Soul awaits no longer.

If you choose to continue to go your old way – then the choice is made. Your decision will be registered according to your actions.

Come, walk with me in the light, the radiance of Soul – *or choose, for your way of being – The Eternal Midnight.*

CHAPTER EIGHT

Evermore – Eternity – Infinity.

When man says these words he means for one what he means for the other. But man has no conception in any way of what *Time* is. Time is not as man thinks it to be. Time is as Soul allows it to be – different in one Universe to another, all-embracing, all-filling. But you will not understand my meaning, nor will you comprehend it until you turn your motives and ways towards value.

Time and understanding.

Man thinks of "understanding" as requiring brain capacity, or perhaps an intelligence quotient or quota, or some sort of natural inborn aptitude. That is why the various occupations and professions require certain tests of intelligence and memory, as you think of it.

Let me now tell you a secret, a fact so alien to your way of thinking and indoctrination that you may not even stop to consider the idea. But it is Truth. The secret is this –

In man *there is no such thing as levels of intelligence – there is no such thing as memory*.

Each and every one of man, except for those with a physically damaged brain, has exactly the same brain capacity, the same ability to understand, as the next man, as the most "brilliant" men in your society today. It is completely wrong and misleading to think of a person as having a certain amount of "brain-power".

The fact of there being no "memory" will be explained to you later, but it is vitally important to realise now, before you go one step further, that every person has the same capacity and opportunity to understand fully all about his own

Universe – so as to make the knowledge that your so-called "expert" scientists claim to possess look like a tiny grain of distorted truth mixed with a cart-load of misleading rubbish – which is just what it is.

You see, the brain does not contain a storage of knowledge and wisdom. The brain does not even make a thought. The brain is merely a "two-way" receiving set, between Soul and Soulpart.

Soul can pass to its Soulparts, to you of man, any thought, idea, item of knowledge or realisation that it wishes. But it sends *only what the Soulpart deserves*. Or what is good for it to use – just what it earns.

In order to begin to receive pure thought and wisdom from Soul, to earn the right to understand all of your own purpose and the Universe you inhabit, all you have to do is to "tune in". After all, even your radio or television set will not receive anything but crackles and noise if you do not take the trouble to tune in and adjust the set properly.

It is so easy.

In order to receive the wisdom and guidance of Soul, the wonderful knowledge of your own Universe, *to become a man inspired,* all you have to do is to tune in. And by that I mean – *to listen to your own Soul in the correct manner.*

Now perhaps you can understand what I mean when I say you will not comprehend the true concept of Time until you turn your motives and ways towards Soul value.

But I will begin to give you just an inkling of the real concept of Time, as an experiment for yourself in understanding. For you may glean an amount of wisdom in this matter from this writing for further consideration and digestion – in exact proportion to the amount of effort you put, not in trying to puzzle out for yourself, but in really *listening to the words of Soul with an open mind*. An open mind. Listening and waiting.

Let me just remind you at this point – I am not as you of man, but my scribe appears as you of man, to you. I am Soul. I see Time. I manipulate Time. *I control Time.* I use Time. I provide Time. Time is not, as man believes, merely an empty measurement of the interval between one happening and the next. Throw out that idea if you wish to come any nearer to the Truth.

Time surrounds you in every direction – it is all-embracing. You are living, existing within that which is Time.

Substance is Time.

I say again that Time is not a measurement. Time contains all substance – substance *is* Time.

As Universes create Power and become fulfilled, then they expand – forever expand, increasingly. *As the Universes expand they cover Time.* It may be likened to a city which grows and grows, and gradually covers a land mass. Time is as that land mass covered. Time is real, is reality, is tangible. But Time to man is not seen, and therefore, in his present state, mis-understood.

To man Time is that which is measured on clocks, the intervals between ticks, between grains of sand dropping. That is not Time, as man will soon find out when Power begins to be produced once more, that those intervals he measures are infinitely variable, not constant as he imagines at present. Clocks and measuring machines will shortly become useless in this respect. It will be like trying to use a ruler to measure the length, or portions of length, of a piece of elastic which is constantly being stretched. Impossible.

I scan the volume of space around me now, away into vast incalcuable distances, and I see nothing – nothing but sub-stance – *only substance spreading everywhere. Everything is substance.*

I see Time.

I look at it as do Souls when they are fulfilled. I look at the substance of space and I decide what goes here and what goes

82

there – the purpose being the filling of space, or I could say – *the fulfilling of space.*

Listen gently and see if you follow my train of thoughts – gradually, a little understanding, a small inkling at a time–but ever so gently. See, if by listening so delicately to the thoughts of Soul, you can pick up the gossamer thread of pure thought and therefore of understanding – just a little, with no impatience. Being content with the tiniest of ideas that Soul sends. That is the way to earn the understanding, the wisdom of Soul, of the Universe. Now listen –

Man performing task – placing "Output" into Earth. Power being produced – transferred to Soul of Universe. Universe becoming fulfilled with Power. Such Universes expanding and fulfilling space – constantly. The Universes cover Time – or, in another way – the covering of the substance that is space, by Universes, by Soul – *that is Time.*

Do not try to comprehend all I say, all I explain to you. You cannot – yet. Soon, if you listen to your own Soul, you will understand all. Merely absorb and wait to see the beginnings of an idea that Soul will send to you. *Be content to begin to understand,* for if you can do just that, you have received the beginnings of *inspiration,* of pure thought from Soul. Then you will go forever forward, never looking back – *if* you are patient, not striving and wanting but content, for the moment, with the first tiny inkling of understanding that Soul sends you.

Time. It is as a pool of water spilt onto a polished surface, spreading out in all directions, at random, as more and more drips of water are added, except that with Soul nothing is random, all is controlled. The pool that is Soul, that is Universes, ever spreads out, but the spreading and direction of spreading is controlled, manipulated by Soul.

Time is controlled completely by Soul.

Time is flexible.

Time never ticks away – but rather can, sort of, be "filled". Do you "hear" what I mean? Relax, and you may do so.

There is one point I have not mentioned specifically in terms of man's concept of Time – past, present, and future.

"Present" does not exist of itself, all is past and future. For example – this moment now . . . . has gone.

It is true to say that Soul sees the future, but more correct to say that Soul "makes" future.

But what of the past? Is the past irreversible and unchangeable? The answer is – No. Generally the principle is that Time can be added to – but never taken away. That is, the Past is not to be altered.

But – the Core of Power changes all, if necessary – though never unless absolutely necessary.

Now, the Core of Power says, that if man does not listen to and follow his own Soul this time – then one section of Time Past will be wiped out as though it had never been.

It will be as though man had never been.

Listen . . .

*　*　*　*　*

Out of time came a new-comer. A man, you could say, that in time he was ancient – as old as the Core of all things. This new-comer to Earth was so very sure that all would be in a better way. The new-comer was a man, and yet not a man – more than a man – much, much more than a man. He was as old as the Core of all things because he was *of* the Core of All, the Core of the Mass of Power. But he came down the ages of time and he stopped at the point in time that you of man call "now".

Now, he is "poised" in thought, in the form of thought, until the right moment, the precise moment.

He comes in the form of thought, as he must in order to enter this Universe of thought. Then, at the precise moment, he will join the cocoon prepared for him, the body ready for him to inhabit during his brief stay upon this Earth. That precise moment will be the moment of the birth of the cocoon. He, a thought, will enter into the cocoon and the cocoon will take its first breath and burst into the crying that signifies life. His life upon Earth in the guise of man has begun.

But it is not just that that he is from the centre of all Power, the Core of Existence. He possesses another quality that is so important to all mankind. He is also the sector of the very Soul of this Universe. He is the Wondrous One.

He is a sector of the Soul of this Universe, of your own Soul, and yet imbued with the very Essence of the Core of Power of the Ultimate.

The new-comer appears, the impetus of life becomes embedded temporarily in the cocoon that he will use. And at that very moment begins the New Age for man – the Age of Enlightenment. The age when all the mysteries of the Universe will be unfolded before the eyes of man, if he cares to look – the age when the voice of inspiration of Soul will speak to every one of man, if he cares to listen.

The dawn of the Golden Age is upon you now – you have only to look around you, you have only to listen in silence.

The new-comer was so sure that all this would come to pass, that all would be in a better way, because he is who he is, and because he came. Because he brings with him the power and authority of the Absolute and because he is the Creator, the Soul of this Universe. Because he is *your* very own Soul, and knows your every feeling, every emotion, every thought – because he sends them to you.

He comes to place before man in no uncertain manner all

the pro's and con's, why's and wherefore's of the situation that man is in now. He comes to tell of "Reality", in simple terms. He comes to make all crystal clear, even to the simplest mind of all – especially to the simplest mind of all. He will show the world such wonders that there cannot be one iota of doubt in one mind of the meaning of the message he brings. He is so certain because he is who he is, and *he knows that HE AND HIS WAY will prevail* – the way of Soul. His way will overcome all. There will be much opposition and battling and struggling against His way – but all will be swept aside.

Their efforts to thwart the way of evolution of Soul will be as effective as a child building sand castles to stem the flow of the incoming tide, or a man puffing out his cheeks in an attempt to blow back against the prevailing wind.

The One who comes will be as a prevailing wind blowing fresh across the face of your Earth – blowing away old ideas, fears, religions, superstitions – blowing away the mask of the ugly face of self of man. Nothing shall withstand it – nothing can.

You of mankind, you have long refused to turn to your own Soul, to the way of Soul, and you have preferred the way of self, of greed and emotion. Now, to make all easy for you, your own Soul comes to you on Earth. Will you recognise in him yourself as you are in Soul? To be sure, he will come as a man, and at first will appear and live as a man-child – having to overcome all the indoctrinations and contaminations that you have experienced. Later he will show himself, in a glory never before seen on Earth.

But first, will you accept a man and his words of Soul, without waiting to be convinced by the coming blaze of glory? Have you the strength, the courage to be one who will prepare the way for him, who will listen and use his own invidual inspiration from Soul to make this world a better place for the Wondrous One to commence his task?

You have a chance to do so.

You have no need to await the might and spectacles of wonder that he will bring, before you become a follower of the Soul of the Universe. You can step forward now and be a leader of men, merely by following your own Soul now.

Then you will be one who has the honour to walk hand in hand with the Wondrous One, and you will share in his glory. You, even you, out of all of mankind, of all places and of all ages, will have the honour to stand beside the Might and Power of the Soul of the Universe, as an equal. From there the reward will be great – for this one act will enable you to make the great leap forward in evolution that would normally take you eons and eons of time. What an honour! What an opportunity of all of your lives! And all you have to do is to be a leader and not a late follower. All you have to do is to step forward with courage now and declare yourself on the side of Soul.

All you have to do is to be there to greet the "Man", the new-comer in a friendly way. When he steps into a hostile world, when all seems against him, and before he reveals his true worth, his true Power – be ready to greet him in the only worthwhile way.

Just tell him – "You are as I" – and he will answer, and his smile will embrace you with all the warmth and peace and adoration of Soul. From that moment you will have earned your place for all time, high in the Realms of Soul – for Soul looks after its own. Soul will place its cloak of care and protection and peace around you – around *you*, leader of men.

The Wondrous One says – "When I come, I will be as man, for at first I shall colour myself pale. But soon the Power and Beauty and Glory of Soul shall blaze forth from me with all the colour of the rainbow, and a thousand times so".

* * * * *

A newcomer came to Earth, down the cone of the ages of time, and he greeted man –

"You are as I," he said.

This newcomer was so sure that all would be in a better way – for he came as the prevailing wind.

Will you have been there to greet him?

You can recognise him by his gentleness.

CHAPTER NINE

The whole way of life of the whole of mankind constitutes an anomaly. By this I mean that their way of life is totally contradictory to their purpose on Earth. Enough of the necessities of life is provided and will be provided by Soul for all those who listen to Soul, and do their best to follow its guidance, to carry out their true task in life. The Force that is Soul will arrange all so that each can live for the sake of Powering his Soul, and of evolving in his own right.

But instead of accepting this situation, most of mankind spends his life using up, burning, destroying that which would provide Power for his Universe. Not only does he waste the peat and coal and oil and gas in his home, but in millions of instances he spends half his waking day in factories and other "jobs", burning the life blood of his very Soul, in order to produce – mostly rubbish.

The anomaly of all anomalies – man comes to Earth and destroys the very Power that he came to make.

He destroys the essence of his being *in order to live* (as he puts it) when he should be living *in order to produce* that which is essential to his continued existence for Eternity. How different all could be – and so easily. Let me show you what I mean.

I see now a young woman, who is standing beside a weaving machine in a filthy, dilapidated old mill in a small town amongst the hills of England. She stands in that same position for a large portion of her conscious life – bored, tired, listless.

She knows no other way to be. She is a virtual prisoner to her job. She has been "conditioned" into believing that she must do this, or some similar thing, in order to have the wherewithal to live – yet she does not know *why* she lives.

It is respectable, acceptable to her society and to her religion, to stand there thus, amid the filth and futility of man – helping to burn the Power that she came to produce for her Soul.

She longs for freedom from this hateful existence – but not once does she listen to the thoughts of her own Soul, not once does she consider that her way of living may be wrong. If she did so, if she was prepared to accept that there was indeed a better way to be, that there was indeed a very important purpose to her life, and that she could discover it by merely opening her mind a little – then her whole life would without doubt change so radically.

Her own Soul would point out to her an easy way to obtain all the necessities of life, and without harming others. She would have guidance every step of the way – the guidance of the very Intelligence of the Universe, no less.

That is all that she would have to do – to listen to the thoughts of her Soul, and then to follow the guidance. So simple. And yet she does not listen, but pursues her purposeless existence in misery, her mind full of worries and problems and anguish, having no security, no peace of mind.

She envies the nomad of the desert lands who is free to roam when and where he pleases, as she imagines. But in reality he is no better off than she is – for he *wanders aimlessly*. He too, is conditioned into thinking that this is his only way of living – for does he not have to keep moving in order to use the sparse pasture and food which he finds for his family and animals? He too imagines that he has to spend most of his waking life merely to find the wherewithal to keep alive, when all the time he could remain in one place, and have enough for all his needs, if only he would stop and listen to the thoughts of his own Soul. No longer would he wander aimlessly, forever searching for he knows not what.

Merely because he stopped and listened would Soul allow him to understand his task in life, and guide him to achieve it

– at the same time as providing all he needed, in an easy way. But he does not stop to listen, and he remains just as much a prisoner to his wanderings as the mill girl is to her machine.

What a truly ridiculous state of affairs! An anomalous situation, man would call it, if he opened his eyes. But I say that it is the height of folly, stupidity almost beyond belief.

But will you believe me, that is the point? Or will you be one of those who will say – "That is all very well to speak about, but who will pay my rent for me, and my grocery bill, if I spend my time finding my purpose in life, even fulfilling my purpose in life? Who will provide for me in a practical way if I spent time listening to my thoughts and trying to be a better person?"

My answer is – "Do you not trust your Self? Would you not trust your own higher Intelligence, which knows all, and which is your very Self? Would you harm yourself?"

Your Soul *is* yourself. Your Soul *is* the Intelligence of the Universe, the creator of all you see around you. Your own Soul is Pure Power and Intelligence, Goodness supreme – and *you* are a part of your Soul. Your Soul sends you every thought you have ever had, every thought that any of man has ever had – every idea or invention, every wise word that was ever uttered. Can you still doubt the ability of your Soul to show you the way to go, to show you the gentle way to obtain all for your needs?

Now begins the Age of Enlightenment. The Age when millions upon millions will learn how to stop what they are doing in such a contradictory way, and listen to the thoughts of wonder and wisdom from Soul. The Age of Man Inspired, when each can receive all by allowing pure inspiration to flow from the Universal Intelligence – *direct* (not through the intermediary of so-called "agents of God").

Millions and millions will do so – and those who refuse to listen, refuse to go the way Soul would guide them will go home to the transit realms, never again to have the chance to come to Earth to try to evolve, to fulfil their set task – the easy way in this Universe. Another way will be theirs in another Universe.

And so, to every question, every objection put forward as to who will provide, how all can possibly come about – the answer is Soul, Soul, and Soul again.

Soul is All.

Each of you would realise that *you are Soul,* have it proved to you beyond all doubt – if you would only listen.

You have nothing to lose – My Way.

You would change a life of anomalies, of contradicting your reason for being, into a life of harmony with the Universe itself.

You have everything to gain – My Way.

And all for the price of a little courage.

Do *you* have what it takes?

You care so much, you of man, for your way – yet where is the happiness, the understanding? You bicker and growl at each other – always someone or something to dislike. What a way to be? You should treat all in a caring way, having no preference for one above another. You will not accept my way – and you only want to go your way. So be it.

But if you could only open your mind to a way so different from yours, then you would have everything of value. But your life is governed by emotion. You are ruled by emotion. You live by it, you swear by it. Emotion. You idolise it, you make a god of it – you make it respectable, acceptable. To you it is unthinkable to live without it. You think, you imagine, you have been well taught, that you would be a "zombie", a walking dead-man without it.

Good and bad emotions. Some emotions you regard as positive and some as negative – therefore some as being desirable, some as undesirable, but unavoidable. You live for your precious emotions – and yet they are not understood at all by you.

You do not know what they are – where they come from, how they come, nor why they come. And yet you are ruled by them. You regard them as "natural" and so you embrace them. You even endow your various Gods with the emotions you deem desirable or suitable. You have "jealous" gods, vengeful gods, gods who "take pity" on man, gods of violence who bless the killers in wars, and even gods who wish you to "fear" them. Jealousy, revenge, pity, violence, fear – all good juicy emotions of man. And how he must like them so, to endow his invented "gods" with them.

But what do they do for you, these emotions? They twist and torture you. They bring you agony of mind and, yes, agony of body too. They turn man against man, causing him to act in an unreasoning manner, an inhuman manner – an annoyed, jealous, vengeful, fearful manner. Liking and disliking, fawning and despising, desiring and repulsing.

Now I put it to you – will you open your mind to the way of another, the ideas of another – to *my way*, to the way of value of Soul? Do you not seek truth unless you can have it in *your way*? Unless it fits in with what you want, or do not want, to give up? Like emotions for instance?

Only the strong will listen to these words, will consider my way with an open mind. Only the strong! The weak will brush aside the way I point out to you – to the accompaniment of many rational excuses, no doubt – all with their attendant emotions.

So now I speak to the strong – to those with the heart of the pioneer, of the true researcher for Truth, of that small fraction of the population who are destined to be leaders – to those who have the courage to be leaders, given half a chance. So now I present you with that chance.

Listen carefully to my words, to the seed of a new idea –

consider it well. Then try it, act upon it, and you will feel the understanding dawn upon you. For true understanding is a gift of Soul, but it is only given when it has been earned, and no amount of pondering and struggling will earn it – only the gentle listening, first to the new idea, the new way to go, then to the gentle voice of Soul within, within your thoughts.

Emotions are unnatural – all emotions. They prevent man from seeing Reality, from understanding all things as they really are. True, some emotions are more harmful to man than others, but *any emotion whatsoever* is sufficient to prevent man from seeing Reality.

All in this Universe is in the form of thought – though it is not always obvious to man. But it is obvious as well as true that all understanding is in the form of thought. Now all understanding, all true knowledge of things as they really are, comes direct from Soul in the form of thought. All thoughts that man considers and uses can either be in their pure form or they can be twisted and distorted and coloured by the time they have filtered through to the active consciousness or awareness of man, any man.

The way of Unreality, which is grey as a drifting mist, you colour with vivid splashes to make it appear bright and gaudy and substantial. Your Soul, who in the realms of Reality is so brilliant and radiant of colour and form, you colour so pale in your own way of thought as to make it appear a nothingness. You reverse all and you fool yourselves.

So we have in man the possibility of pure unadulterated thought, which is the key to all wisdom and understanding on Earth, the essence of "inspiration", or of distorted and coloured thought, the thought of illusion, of unreality. Unreal because it does not show things as they really are.

But what is the difference, how does the difference come about? What causes this difference in the mind between pure thought and thoughts of unreality, of distortion? The answer can be given in one word – and that word is *"Emotion"*.

In his present condition and to his never-ending misery, man never is able to make use of pure thought, of inspiration, of wisdom, of understanding of reality. Life is so difficult for man on Earth because he has no sense of reality. Whatever he tries to do for self is as blind and distorted and false as the thoughts that he embraces and uses. And the thoughts which he embraces and uses are not related to reality because they are mixed with and governed by his beloved emotions. But man is not willing to let go of them – Rather like a man trying to swim across the current of a deep river, clutching and weighted down by bags full of shiny but heavy metal, which he regards as precious. He can barely keep his head above water, and mostly doesn't, but he struggles and kicks and wails for help and all but destroys himself – all rather than even considering letting go, letting go of the bags of rubbish which drag him down to the depths, so much value does he place upon them and their shiny contents.

Such is man in life, clinging to his destructive emotions – forgetting that his purpose is to cross the stream, and thinking that it is to hang on to the gold, the glittering and killing trinkets, which are his emotions. Yes, man certainly does make all life on Earth difficult for himself, for he gropes in the distorted world of self-delusion and plays with things which are all unreal. He pushes aside understanding.

Where is your happiness, you of man, where is your joy in living, your purpose in life? Where is your peace of mind? I see before me only billions of wasted and wasting lives. Man does not care for his own Soul in any way, for his creator, for the Intelligence of the Universe. He cares only for what *he* wants, for going where his precious emotions tell him he should go. And he has been doing this, going the way dictated by emotion, for millions of years – but where has it led him? Into one struggling, tortured, morass of pain and bewilderment – of unreality.

Let me give you an idea. Take my hand, in thought, and let me take you up the first step of freeing yourself from your slavery to the god of emotion. Consider this way. The aspects of emotion represented by anger and annoyance.

Not only does man not care for Soul, but he rejects the caring which Soul sends to him, that which could be the understanding of all, were it well received. He rejects this caring for him by Soul because he wants only what *he* wants, never seeing the beauty in Soul, never glimpsing the peace, the Truth, that which is reality. Man rejects. *He wants his own way – in all things.*

All annoyance and anger stems from not being able to have his own way. Annoyance and anger – then resentment, violence, hatred, jealousy, dislike, discontent, fear – and many, many more aspects. And all because man cannot get his own way. *His* own way.

Now. Stop. Consider. Consider my way. There is no other way to go, only the way of value of Soul, the way of no emotion. Try it. It is easy once you do it. Then you will understand all, know all of your own Universe, enjoy all.

Life is for enjoying, doing and enjoying – in spite of what the religious "holy joes" tell you.

Let me show you how to get rid of all emotion. Let me show you how to replace it with Soul feelings, Soul senses – *in the natural way*. Let me show you how to begin to enjoy life, to have calmness and peace of mind. Take my way. Believe me, it is easy. It is only the way of emotion that is hard.

No one asks you to be a "zombie", to inhabit an empty unfeeling shell of a body. On the contrary, the way of no emotion but of Soul feeling shows you how to become so sensitive to all around you, so delicately feeling, so alive, alert, aware – as you have never been before in your Earth life.

A hand that is coursened by hard skin and segs, through fighting or wielding a pick or shovel, can never feel or appreciate the difference between silks and satins and other fine materials. A delicate or well-cared-for hand can do this – can enjoy the sense of touch to the full – can *understand* much more about all it encounters by direct experience, in a way that a calloused and insensitive hand never can.

So it is with the perception and sensitiveness of the mind. The one bred on the coarseness of the emotions of man can feel only that which is coarse and rough to handle. It misses so much. Much that is within its grasp that passes between its fingers, it fails to "see" or understand. It rejects what is of value, what is of beauty – it grasps what is ugly, and abrasive, and worthless.

This is exactly how it is with you of man at present. Soul sends you so much of value, so much caring – but you reject it, you throw it away as being valueless. You don't see it or feel it or understand it. You waste it, you destroy it. All because your love of emotion has made you so, has made you incapable of seeing Soul, of seeing the beauty of Soul, of enjoying Soul – of seeing how life can be, the beauty of life – of enjoying all.

In your everlasting wanting, wanting things as *you* want them to be, you lose all. For then you engender your ugly emotions of anger and annoyance at not getting your own way, which you imagine is so precious and so beneficial to you.

Look at yourselves and see how you hate and dislike people and things that do not go *your* way. See all the discord and strife around you. Be wise and see all the joy and happiness slipping away unnoticed and unwanted. Stop your ugly wanting, stop your emotions now. Stop your ugly emotions and allow the pure thought of Soul to come to you, the pure intelligence that is yours by right, the understanding of reality.

Be content no longer with the turmoil and illusion of distorted and falsely coloured thought. Accept peace of mind, tranquillity. With a little practice, a little caring, your mind can become so sensitive once more to all that is of value. But caring you do need to be. Caring of your own wonderful and mighty and intelligent Soul, and caring of your fellow beings – man and beast.

Then you will find that *you* can live in harmony with *all* – all of man and all of the Universe – whether others care to be in harmony with you or not.

It happens that way. Try it. It is not so difficult. In fact – you will have never tried any way of being that is more natural – emotionless but with Soul feeling – for that is how you are in Soul.

You are as I in Soul – you could be so on Earth – in this way.

Purposelessness. The curse of mankind. The disease that has been contracted by every one of man. The plague that is passed on to each new-born child as it arrives on Earth. Result – chaos.

Organised chaos to be sure, for man is so very good at organising others. So good at it! He regimentates, schools, marshalls, trains, orders, segregates, disciplines, regulates, governs – in so many different ways of organising others to do what he wants them to do. But all to no avail, all to no real purpose.

Man does not know his purpose, he has no idea of his ultimate destination – that is the reason why he allows himself to be led so easily, hoping that the ones who step forward to organise him know where he is going. But no, these arrogant ones are merely using his fear and uncertainty, his insecurity, to further their own ends – of love of power, of greed, of prestige.

Man looks down upon a colony of ants, and he sees chaos there – a seemingly unruly, disordered milling-about with no set end in view. Man is so wrong.

Each tiny ant is in perfect contact with his Soul, and is carrying out his individual and collective purpose in life, and in so doing he is co-operating, though not interfering with his fellows. Each knows his purpose and will not be shaken from it. That is why, in Soul home, they are so highly evolved – far more so than man.

Soul looks down and sees millions of ant-like men, scurrying and rushing, crawling like a seething mass across the face of their Earth. Never still, always moving goods and produce and their own bodies from place to place, country to country – always in a frantic haste. Chaos. Nearly always these tiny figures are in ranks and files and lines, as they cart their useless manufactured items around, or march to destroy their fellow creatures – all futile. A highly organised futility – but still futile. Soul sees the chaos and Soul is not mistaken.

Man does not listen to his Soul. He travels fast and furious, without knowing his destination – without realising his destiny.

Some of man move about merely because they do not see any reason for being or remaining where they are. It is a form of discontent. Their life, the way it is, does not satisfy them. How can it? – for they do not know what life is all about.

Others travel in order to sun themselves in more pleasant climes or surroundings, but after a while they find themselves no better off than they were before, because they are wanting still further changes.

Others travel about the Earth for "reasons of trade" – they find places wherein to buy, sell, and exchange their goods, as they think of them. So much do they love to do this, that motor vehicles produced in country A are sold to another land on the opposite side of the world, whilst *their* motor vehicles, almost identical, are transported and sold back to country "A" – sometimes literally tens of thousands of miles away. Millions of large coloured tin boxes with wheels being dragged around the world, at great wastage of resources, labour, and power, to places perfectly capable of making their own, or even doing without them. Motive – greed.

On the other hand, there are nations with large stock piles of rotting food who, because of their stupid regulations would rather allow it to go bad or dump it, than sell it to a neighbour who has urgent need of such. Motive – greed.

Man does have other reasons for travel. I see vast armies and small armies of men marching over many areas of your land space, from man-made boundary to man-made boundary. Their motive to subdue, suppress, kill, maim, torture, burn, and bully others of man. A man is taught so thoroughly how to march in step with his brother by his side and to obey any orders given, unthinkingly, automatically, puppet-like – and how to pull a trigger and injure or kill his brother who happens to live on the other side of the fence – who is also organised and obeys orders like a puppet on a string. Motive? – perhaps unknown to the cannon-fodder – the greed and power-lust of their controllers.

"Travel broadens the mind" say the closed-minded ones who have travelled. That is so that they may appear more knowledgeable than their fellows. So, believing this, many of man go journeying to see the sights, the see how others live, hoping to gather culture, wisdom, knowledge of what the world is about. Some go to study other religions, or find "gurus" or spiritual guides who can sell them understanding of the purpose of life. Many, many take their money – none can deliver the goods – simply because they do not possess them. They only pretend. As for learning wisdom from observing the ways of life of others of other lands – this too is impossible, for those of other lands are in just as much of a mess of non-understanding of life and its purpose, as the travellers are.

You have of course the travellers, the seekers after what they imagine they do not possess themselves, but who do *not* move about the surface of the Earth – the arm-chair travellers, the book readers. They follow the journeyings and seekings of others, because they are unable to go for themselves, but their purpose may be the same.

Looking down from the vantage point of Soul upon your Earth, I see its surface teeming with a minute form of life – a restless, ever moving mass of ant-like creatures, all moving around in an often well-ordered, ever changing, yet patternless form of chaos. *I see purposelessness.* I see the seething mass.

And again, when I look closer, I focus on the individual, and I see a man struggling for understanding of the true way to go. I see a man looking desperately for a purpose – a purpose beyond greed, power, wealth, prestige. *I see him searching for his true purpose.* I see the individual looking for a warmth that he cannot find in the sun, for a wisdom that he cannot find in exotic religions, and "holy wise men". I observe him seeking for a way to evolve and progress, that he cannot find in science and technology. I see the individual desperately scanning libraries of books, looking for an answer to the mysteries of the Universe – the mystery of the purpose of life.

Wherever I focus close-up on the teeming millions of ant-like creatures, always frantically scurrying, I pick out the lonely one who is rushing about also, and has cast his line into the turmoil, angling, fishing, for his understanding *in the way of outward looking*, instead of calmly standing still and netting the true way of Soul thoughts, within. It is to the individual that Soul now speaks, not to the senseless, leader-less, purposeless mass. Soul does not deal with, nor recognize, masses of mankind. No one of man has ever been authorised nor is capable of ordering or organising the life of another, let alone of thousands, or millions of others. *Soul speaks to individual man, direct.* It sends him all thoughts of guidance, of wisdom, of understanding of life and life's purpose, if he will but listen – for himself.

Man, lonely man – alone among the struggling morass of mankind – I send you this thought, this message through the media of one who is not of you. I say to you to stop searching among other peoples and other places. Stop milling around in circles with the mobs, who maraud like headless, brainless monsters – merely destroying their environment and eventu-ally themselves and others. Step outside of the chaos created by witch-doctors and priests in mud huts and palaces, of medicine men and experts in fine feathers and plush offices, of battle-chiefs who lead the killings from the front and ministers-for-defence who lead the killings from the rear.

Lonely man, step outside all of this. Stop your running to and fro, stop looking at others for your answers and solutions to your questions and problems. They do not have them. Your own Soul has the answer to all, and so have you if you will only stand still and listen. You, your Soul, are your own "expert", medicine man, priest, and leader. *You have all, if you care to use it.*

Lonely man, no need now to desperately seek a trustworthy partner, one who will never let you down, one who is worthy of your absolute confidence, one who is the higher intelligence of the partnership. *You have it.* The best partner any man could ever wish for.

Lonely man, you no longer have a need to travel, to search for the warmth of the sun, combined with the cool of the shade – the warmth and the balm of true companionship.

A companion who will look to you, who will consider your needs, regardless of self, constantly. *You have such a companion*, if you will allow it to embrace you. Open your minds, your arms to your higher self, to your own wonderful and caring Soul – then feel the warmth and the glow, the elevating companionship and security of Soul embrace you, surround you like a shield against all the ugliness and harm of the true hell that you now inhabit, that man has created for himself.

Weary traveller, now rest – wherever you are, stop and rest – rest deep in the warmth and the cool of the tranquillity within. Repose. Cease your hopeless journeyings, your running, your futile searching, all you need, all your nature requires, the satisfaction of all your longings – is within. It lies within the depths of the pool of the tranquil mind. No need now to go further. Your Soul says so.

I tell you now the words of your own Soul. Listen to them, consider them, and treasure them – for it is in reality your own true self who speaks. Then, listen to your own thoughts for yourself.

"Lonely man, you so are as I. You are I. Part of Self whom I have set upon the Earth to carry out a task on my behalf – I adore you. You are, in truth, more than precious to me, regardless of self. You are of me. I open my arms to you, I invite you. I have all for you – all comfort, all protection, all peace of mind, the answer to all your longings.

Why do you continue to stagger around under your self-imposed burden, travelling furiously yet wandering aimlessly. Merely come to me in thought. Thought is so powerful. Thought can alter, can overcome all. I make thought and I am waiting to send you all your needs in thought – thought to be transformed into fact, substantial fact.

I await you.

You are I. Now allow me to give to you – your share of *all*. I can tap the Source of all Power, all Wisdom of the Universes, for I am linked to the Ultimate. I await for you to accept and to evolve and inherit the full glory of your own Universe. Listen to me in thought.

Let me show you your destiny, allow me to lead you, to guide you to it. The stars are yours, if you will but reach out in thought to me – for *I am the stars*. And I am you. You are as I.

Why ride facing rearwards on the back of a crazed donkey, never knowing where you are going or why? – when you could with ease soar to the beauty of the heavens and to the fulfilment of your own destiny – merely by listening to the thoughts of wonder, of wisdom, that I would send you.

Lonely traveller, come to me!

After all, *we are one – you and I*."

CHAPTER TEN

The Spiral that is a Universe constantly turns – the Spiral that is in the shape of an inverted cone. When a Universe is first formed it is given a boost of Power from the Mass which will keep it going until the Universe becomes fulfilled and produces sufficient Power of its own to turn itself.

Power must have a way of movement, and that movement must be in accordance with a pattern or beat. It must be a rhythm, a pulsing. When it ceases to do this it is lifeless, dead – it is no longer Power.

The Power that is Soul pulsates, the Power of the Universe beats out a rhythm, the life that is on your Earth vibrates to a pattern – the Essence of the being that is man also pulses. Even the body that that being (you yourself) inhabits – pulses. When it no longer does so the cocoon no longer exists as a unit, and it disintegrates into lifelessness.

The life-beat of the Power of the Soul of this Universe is now faint within man – his pulse is weak. The outward rhythm which he contrives to have is now *jerky* – it is a rhythm out of control. This jerkiness is in all of man's movements – except when he throws himself into a state of complete listlessness – which he regards as relaxation. This outwards way of moving of man is the opposite of *grace,* which man of this civilisation possesses in no way at all.

When man dances he often hypnotises himself into his own way of pulsating. Chanting can have a similar effect and religion, in all its forms, uses both aspects within its rituals – for its own purposes. Over the centuries the pulsing of the body of man diminishes in beat, because no longer does any Power flow into it in a valuable way from its own Soul. There is only that which is required to keep it ticking over.

Man is tired. His movements are no longer smooth, grace-ful, effortless – they are fast, jerky, and straining. Man is "running down" like an unwound clock. He drifts towards oblivion – self annihilation. Man requires more sleep now then ever before in his five million years of existence on Earth – sleep, not to replenish his energy, for he has almost nil of that, but merely to give sufficient to stabilise him. When tired the balance goes and one begins to easily fall over. Therefore, jerkiness – no grace.

Gone are the ages when man had such energy poured into him that in body he could practically glide along effortlessly, whilst in mind he was so alert and keen of thought that he could cut through any obstacle like a knife through butter. That was a state of Energy – Power of Soul.

He pulsed with energy – he radiated the Essence of life. The body of man actually *shone*, and the glow of vitality of the Essence of life radiated from him.

Man of today, of the tail-end of a played-out Universe, all that remains of a Power-starved Earth – is tired and listless. He is drab and practically lifeless by comparison. He needs to spend one third of his life in sleep, in order to be able to with-stand his way of feeble and strange movement, during the other two thirds. What a pathetic state to be in!

Normally, a Universe begins to produce Power of its own almost immediately – after the first one thousand years or so. It does this by means of its Earth – the dynamo of the Uni-verse, which produces Power to turn the Spiral as required and to fulfil the Universe, so that eventually it no longer re-quires the dynamo of Earth, but is self-sustaining.

The Planets, billions of them, first of all travel "down" from the head of the Universe, between the two outer "skins" of the Universe, entering at the base to fulfil their task of receiv-ing the Power produced by the Earth. Once full of Power, they then place themselves on a "track" of the Spiral. The movement of the turning of the Spiral forces them outwards along the track, which ever widens, and therefore upwards at the same time. Thus the Power is transported to the head of the Universe. This process continues until the Universe is fulfilled with Power.

But the turning of the Spiral also serves to stabilise all within the Universe – all upon the Earth. Also, the Universe pulses, because the Power of the Soul of the Universe pulses. All that is within the Universe pulses – all that lives upon the Earth, too, has its own beat – including each Soulpart and the cocoon occupied by each Soulpart. All the movement and all the pulsing within the Universe is in harmony – smooth, unhurried, rhythmic, effortless. But there is one exception – this Universe of yours.

It is now five million years since the creating of this Universe, and the boost of Power originally given to it by the Mass has been used up. It has been far too long in coming to fulfilment. The Power is not being produced by this Earth of yours. It is not a dynamo but a dead weight on the end of a pendulum. The beings that are on Earth for the express purpose of producing Power for the Soul – do not do so.

They are as parasites eating away the life of the Universe and giving nothing.

The Universe is not as the experts say (who can see only one small area of the base) expanding – it is contracting at a very fast rate. It is shrivelling, closing in upon itself. At the moment it has to be sustained by a supply of Power direct from the Core of All. Even the now-faint beat within the being of man has to be supplied by the Core. You of man of this Earth have drained your own Soul dry of Power, even to the task of maintaining its own Soulparts. It has to be replenished by the Mass in order to remain the being of might of Power and Intelligence that it still is.

The Spiral of your Universe is at a standstill – it no longer turns. All within the Universe is off-balance, and the essential functions have temporarily to be manoeuvred by the Soul direct. The pulse has slowed, man staggers, the forces of "nature", of Soul, about your planet, are off-balance and seem hostile to man. The elements roar or burn, or drown, the Earth itself cracks and erupts. Man suffers – suffers the consequences of his own actions. He ignores the way his own Soul points, ignores his own Soul. He does not even listen.

When the beat of the being that is man becomes strong once again, when the Spiral of the Universe begins to turn once again, when the "elements" become in-balance once again – then man and all the life and mechanism of the Universe, *will be in harmony*. Man at last will be at peace, he will be quiet in mind. He will be *natural*. All his worries and cares, his hardships and his problems, will dissolve – for these are merely the clashings and disharmonies of the varied pulses and patterns of the elements of the Universe, when they lack the Power to pulse with their true beat, as was intended.

Look around and observe for yourself from the clues that I give you. If you walk too slowly, you tend to over-balance – the same applies to riding a bicycle.

When your pulse beats slower you become tired and sleepy (not the reverse as your scientists believe), and your thought is not clear and alert.

When your pulse is really slow and you lose consciousness (sleep) then the body becomes colder.

Your Earth is in a state of slumber – no heat is produced from it, there are even ice-caps over large areas. The Earth should be warm constantly all over – but its pulse is faint. *The dynamo is all but stopped.*

When the Spiral turns, the planets pass close to the Earth in turn, collect the Power from the moon as it leaves the rim of the Earth's atmosphere, and pass on higher up the Spiral towards the head of the Universe. Now they stand still in this respect queueing for the Power that never comes, and you see the same ones century by century.

Notice that the beat from music enters into the *ear* – that the stronger the beat, the more rousing the music, the more alert and lively the mind and body becomes. Notice too, that the organ of balance of the body is located in the region of the *ear*. Many peoples who do not have music, only drums, drum themselves into a state of stupor with a consistant beat. All music, chanting, and drumming is an attempt to replace the beat that man all but lacks. But it is not a beat from within, and not one that will put him in harmony with his Universe with his Soul.

If you really look, you will see that all is connected with the pulsing of the Soul of the Universe. Not only the "solar system" turns, as man says, but the very Universe itself.

If you really listen within, in your thoughts, you will be able to hear your own beat – not your heart beat, but the pulsing of your own Soul. But this will only come about if your intention is to use all for the benefit of your fellow men, not for self in any way. Remember you cannot fool Soul, who sends your thoughts. He who follows his Soul, that one will hear loud and clear, and all the benefits of harmony with All will come his way – that is an absolute certainty. In the true sense will he inherit the Earth, the goodness of it.

Pulsing balances all. Through it comes the voice of Soul so clearly. Clear thought, pure thought – that is the voice of Soul.

* * * * *

It is clear that there are only two ways to go for mankind. Either he keeps on his present course of collision with destruction – the clashing with his own nature and with the pattern and pulsing of his Universe – or else he listens to the Voice of his Soul, and begins to fulfil the pure purpose of his existence – to Power the Soul of his Universe. The first way can only lead to man's annihilation, and to a continual worsening of his lot, right up to the final moment of the total collapse of his Universe. The second way will bring him undreamed-of benefits, the first step on the road to evolving in his own right.

But what prevents man from fulfilling his purpose of producing Power? There are several reasons. Firstly, up to this moment during this era, he has not known of his Soul, of the state of his Universe, of his true purpose on Earth – therefore he has not known the way to go.

Next, he has not known how to listen to his own Soul, to be guided by it – because from birth he has been indoctrinated at every turn into religions, rituals, Society rules and customs, and invented "morals" – different in various areas of the world. He has been given no chance to think freely for himself, but has been told "this is right" and "this is wrong". He has been brought up to believe that all emotions are natural and proper. That it is right to react in this way or that, with anger or pity, or violence, merely because another speaks against what the first one has been taught to believe. Or that it is right to kill his fellow men in wars, if his religion or country tells him to do so.

He has been taught that if he does not look after self first, protect self – then he will "go under". Self is paramount within all.

Man has been taught to "own" or possess other beings, including man, in many ways – also to become a prisoner himself, with duties to conform to the ways or likes or dislikes of others. Yet he prevents others and himself from following his own intended pattern in life by this way of possession and encroachment – in marriage, families, schools, religions, and so on.

The main items keeping man from his purpose in life are – indoctrination, possession, selfishness, ignorance of truth, emotions (especially violent and negative ones), and most of all, religions.

I must stress again that I am not of man, even though the cocoon I use has lived as man, and appears to be as man in body and in past ways. I am not even of this Universe, but I have been sent to your Earth with the one single objective, the one task. It is my mission to bring to you the knowledge and understanding of your own Universe and its workings, of your Earth and its function, of your Purpose in life, and of who you are. I come to tell you of your own mighty Soul and of what you could become, if you cared to do so.

My task is to warn you of the annihilation which stares you in the face now, in the immediate future, if you refuse to fulfil your own Destiny.

I come, not to interfere with man in any way, but to point out the way to go if he is to survive. I can show you the "how" of the ways to your own Soul and to glory. But I am one of many such beings from other Universes, I am one of thousands, who come with the strength and Intelligence of their own Universe, their own Soul behind them.

We are planted in all places of Earth, all walks of life, all colours and races. But we are here and about to reveal ourselves in no uncertain manner.

Have no fear, we are not here to harm or to force man in any way. It is against our way to encroach upon another, to force our way upon him. We merely state how all is and leave to each individual Soulpart of Earth the choice – to follow their Destiny, or to reject, and discover for themselves the consequences.

Those who wish to follow their own Soul, we embrace and guide and protect – against all the upheavals to come. Soul always protects all who make the effort to find Truth and follow it when found.

But this army of Souls which is amongst you now – is here

to prepare the way for a very special one – not one of another Universe, but an Ambassador of the Soul of *this* Universe. It is the Wondrous One who comes, and he will have flowing through him the Power and Wisdom of the Core of All – the Absolute of all the Universes and more.

The Wondrous One is here now upon your Earth. He is your own Soul, now waiting to grow as a man, to guide you to a better way. *He* is the one who has come down the cone of the ages of time. *He* is the prevailing wind. *He* is the one hope of mankind. *He* is the one *who is as you.*

Accept him. Embrace him. Let him draw you to him. Recognise your own Soul, and in that same cocoon, recognise the Power and Intelligence of the Core of All.

Too late to stop him now – he is here.

Too late to destroy him – he is indestructible.

Too late to stop others from hearing of his Truth – *His* Voice will penetrate to all and brook no interference.

Too late to fight against the prevailing wind – the gentle breeze is already born and the natural forces of the Universe are ranged alongside.

Fight this One, and you fight the might of a billion Universes. Choose your side now. Have the courage to stand alongside those of the lands of Soul. With them, help to prepare the way to greet the Wondrous One.

Listen to the wonder of the Voice of your own Soul – and allow it to guide you.

Then you can say, in Truth, to the new-comer of your own Soul – You are as I.

Go into annihilation if you *wish*.

Come towards what I offer you, if you *care*.

Glory awaits you who recognize Truth when you see it.

You too can be as I in Eternity.

The Choice is Yours.

CHAPTER ELEVEN

There is a certain Essence of Soul which is so vital to your existence as separate individuals on this Earth. Your physical bodies are impregnated with this Essence, within the tissues of the skin. It is the Essence that is given from the Mass of Power to Soul to form *shape*.

All beings have shape of some sort, and such is the nature of substance that each being, or even object, would simply merge into the surrounding substance or into each other, were it not for the controlling influence of that Essence.

All substance is constantly moving, weaving, merging – and the only objects or bodies which remain the same in shape are those which are set in that way with this Essence. It is called Malgum.

Your body, for instance, has a constant swirl of substances passing directly through it, as well as other substances around which cannot penetrate. But if it were not for Malgum, then the body would lose its shape and gradually intermingle with other substance, and so disintegrate. Each living body or plant on Earth is set with a certain quantity of Malgum, and that is what determines the length of time that the body or plant retains its shape before decaying.

Each Soul, on receiving the Essence that is Malgum from the Core of the Mass agrees on its own type of shape for its beings – but each Soul differs from the next in this choice, even though only a little at times. No two Universes are allowed to have beings of exactly the same shape, and all are distinguishable by their own shape.

On your Earth, for example, it would be impossible for a being in the shape of man to change or develop into the shape of chimpanzee, for his shape has been defined by the setting of Malgum in his Soul. (So much for the *theory* of Evolution of man from monkeys and slugs).

It is important to be clear that Malgum is a part of the Mass which holds at bay all the substances that would erode the substance of the body, and so cause its disintegration. In a cruel age of a past civilisation, much more advanced than yours of today, man discovered a way that would dissolve the bone structure of the body, so turning the victim into a living jelly. But they could never understand why nothing they did would dissolve the shape of the body. He had thought that the flesh of the body was merely formed around the bone skeleton rather than the bones forming within the confining shape. Man is able to mar the shape of a being, by cutting or stitching or even burning flesh – but he will never be able to see or detect what it is that holds the shape together – not until he becomes a Soul in his own right, that is.

The action of Malgum is simple – it holds what man calls the tissue of the body supple against the harshness of the atmosphere substance. Just take a look at ulcerated flesh or running sores, which will not allow the skin tissues to grow over them, and you can have an idea of how the body would be without Malgum, which is set within the skin.

Tissue needs Malgum, and Malgum is the Essence of Soul. Flesh is intended for a particular purpose, and the amount of Malgum inserted into the flesh before the being is born onto a particular Earth, is decided by the task that lies ahead.

There is only one possible source of the substance that is Malgum – it is produced by the utilisation of the Power of the Mass. This is the only place and method of production of the Essence within all the lands of Soul, and it is not because the Mass fears that it may be misused by others, if they were free to do so. It is true that some within Soul upon an Earth could cause a slight amount of disruption, for all are constantly given free choice – but that is not the reason for restricting the making of Malgum to one source. The simple reason is that only the Core of All can do it, and even the Core is not aware of any other place or area where it can be done. Those of areas of lands other than those of Soul, have a different means of holding shape – within their own substance.

Shape plays such an important part in the system of things, not only upon your Earth, but also in the realms of Transit in which all Soulparts have their home up to the fulfilment of their task on Earth.

A Soulpart can split itself up into several sections, within itself – with each section of the same shape and yet interlocking with every other one, to form the whole – which outwardly remains unchanged, a magnificent being. Under normal circumstance, there would be no need for a Soulpart to sub-divide itself, for it would merely, as a whole, pay just the one visit to the Earth of its Universe, complete its task, and then pass on to the higher realms of Soul.

It would have earned its evolvement by caring to carry out its Earthly function of making Power for its own Soul, and for the benefit of its fellow Soulparts. That would be the one act of caring necessary to shoot it forward to begin its evolution towards Soul.

In the situation which exists on your Earth today – and over the last four million years – real caring is a quality of which man has been completely devoid. Man does not even know *how* to care. But Soulparts must learn how to apply caring in order to evolve. In almost all cases, except that of a newly-formed Soulpart, the Soulpart splits itself into a small group of sectors which it sends down to the Earth.

Looking at the overall conditions on Earth from the Transit Realms, the Soulpart sets down the sectors so that they are able to interact in such a manner as to be able to practise, mostly upon one another, all aspects of caring. These sectors may be a close group of family or friends, either male or female, or may be individual leaders in differing fields or different races or nations.

Whatever the positioning of the sectors, Soul will arrange that their paths cross in some way, if they do not reside close together.

It is highly probable that you yourself are a part of a group which, upon returning to Soul, will interlock to form one whole, *one being, one consciousness.*

Another way of saying this, is that you have other parts of *yourself* around you in some way. Allow me to give you an example.

A particular Soulpart may decide that it can best put into practise all aspects of caring by dividing itself into, say, ten sectors to place upon the Earth. Five of those are to be orphans in an institution, three of them teachers or staff, and two others patrons or managers of the orphanage. Two of the orphan children may be "soft" or "cry-baby" types – two may be naughty types at one stage – and the fifth may be almost blind, but not sufficiently so to be taken elsewhere. The two "patrons" may be so wealthy as to be able to make the lives of the children quite pleasant and comfortable if they cared. One or two of the three teachers or "staff", may be keen on "discipline", that is, exerting power over others for its own sake, and so have the capacity to make the lives of the children a misery if they so wished.

You can visualise all the varying ways that all members of the group of sectors could act upon the others. There would be so many ways of practising *caring* towards all the others – or so many ways of practising *cruelty*, for free choice is forever present. But they would, in reality, be practising the way that they chose – *upon themselves.*

How ironic, how disastrous for the group to go back home to the realms (perhaps at different times), then to rejoin together and become the one Soulpart, only to find that it had been hating and ill-treating its very self, preventing itself from fulfilling its purpose in life – causing itself so much anguish in Reality by being *uncaring* for what it thought were others of man, during its lifetime on Earth.

Look around you! Do you know which of those you know and have dealings with are in reality your very self? Look for those you have "love-hate" relationships with, those you have power over, or those who control you in some way. They could even be your counter-parts in other lands, expecially if you are a leader of some sort – just as some powerful war-leaders of different nations have been sectors of the same Soulpart in recent times, even though they incited the killings from opposite sides. It would be rather like a person making letter-bombs which blind and maim, and then having a helper who picks out random names and addresses from a public direc-tory, and therefore sending a bomb unknowingly to himself which will cripple and blind him. In Soul, *you yourselves* arrange that you pay for all the evil that you do. Those particular war leaders that I mentioned are now in the Universe of the Wise One, paying for their heinous crimes against mankind, against Soul – but they have not yet been re-joined as one unit, for they will have to live out eons of time in the separate roles of the ones that they were on Earth, until they are sufficiently evolved to once again become one Soulpart.

At first it may appear to be "unjust" that the whole group of a Soulpart should suffer for the sake of some of its members, but this is not so. It is always arranged that if even one sector of a Soulpart chooses to go the way of caring for its fellows in the best way that it knows how, then all the other sectors of the group which form the same Soulpart, are given the same understanding, and will change their ways from evil to caring.

This is the vitally important point to bear in mind. If even one member of a Soulpart grouping, which is in Reality just one being, chooses to constantly act in a caring way towards its fellows – then it has been arranged that all other members of that group will change to a caring way. The efforts of one part of that being are sufficient to save the entire being, split into several parts, from helping to destroy itself.

You could be the cause of many others taking a way of caring towards yourself and their fellow beings – merely by changing to that way yourself. No need to try to change others – Soul arranges all. Otherwise, be careful whom you hate or ill-treat. It is highly likely to be your very self.

In the Reality of Soul you, a complete Soulpart, are a truly glorious being – now, be as you really are.

* * * * *

Beyond the hill there exist other beings – aliens in every way – they are pushing, probing, building up pressure by sheer weight of numbers. They are leaning hard on the barrier that separates them from us, and each moment they become stronger and more persistent. As long as they exist they will never cease to try, in all ways possible, to overrun the lands of Soul, and all surrounding areas of substance, until they have smothered all life within those areas – and within Our Lands. They are the Invaders – the Mindless Ones.

Already they have overrun five other areas of substance and wiped out all trace of the beings that were within. There is no means of communicating with them, for they have no controlling Intelligence now, as they once had in a by-gone age. All methods of communication have been tried repeatedly – and failed. They are indeed the Mindless Ones.

Other "dimensions" there are beyond our boundaries, beyond the Mindless Ones, whose beings are so weirdly different from us and from the Invaders. Yet they have evolved into a way of caring for what is within them and for others.

In particular there are those of the area directly adjoining the Invaders – and they are such gentle ones, so delicate. But already a part of their area of substance is occupied by the Mindless Ones, and they are crushed into the remaining space in a cruel fashion. So much destruction has already been done to them that, in a way, they gasp for the life-giving substance that they need in order to exist. But the substance of their space has been pressed so solid that they can almost no longer take from it what they need.

At one stage, the Core of the Mass of Power probed and looked into other areas, and saw that the Invaders were pushing in a solid wall of beings into the Lands of these caring ones. Seeing how utterly defenceless they were, the Mass experimentally sent into that area of alien substance a wall of Power to confront the Invaders. It worked – the Power from the Core of the Mass held back the creeping menace of the Invaders.

At first the caring ones did not know what was happening, and when their Controlling Intelligence was contacted it accepted gratefully the protection of the Power of the Mass. Since then the progress of the Mindless Ones has been checked by the barrier of Power, but the amount of life-force that the Caring Aliens can extract from their substance in its present condition is dwindling fast.

Already the Core has given quantities of the Essence of itself, which has been used to transform part of the alien substance into a state which they themselves can handle and so extract their life-force. Now, amounts of the Essence of the Core, Power, have been given more and more frequently, and soon a continuous supply will have to be kept up, if the Caring Ones are to survive.

Many other types of beings of other dimensions or areas of substance, have already joined us – joined us in alliance against the mindless Evil Ones, who forever press forward on all fronts.

Whatever made the Mass originally, made it as an experimental item – a non-living device, a "robot" you might say, made to serve a purpose. It was quite unaware that it had endowed it with a certain Essence, which gave it awareness of self and the capacity for independent action. That certain something was *Intelligence*, and it was this that made the Mass of Power into a *living* mass.

Its maker destroyed itself in the creation of the Mass, and passed over to it a part of its Intelligence. Now the beings, which were once an integral part of the maker of the Mass, are lacking any Intelligent Controller or any individual intelligence. They forever continue to perform only what they have been "programmed" to do, the most important factor of which is dividing themselves.

It is ironic that what was intended to be a mere mindless robot by its maker, turns out to become billions of super-intelligent living beings, whilst the maker turns itself into billions of mindless "robots".

The Essence of Caring, of giving, was instilled into the Mass from its very beginning – in the form of Intelligence. Caring and giving is as natural to the Mass as breathing is to you. Caring is merely the application of Intelligence. It cannot be otherwise – for survival in its true state depends upon caring. Imagine how vital it would be for Siamese twins, who share the same heart, to care each for the health of the other. Intelligence dictates it to be so.

Caring means giving to others and it is the nature of the Mass to do so. It is *your* natural way in Soul.

The Mass is a Power-producing unit by nature, and when it gives of its Power to beings outside of itself – both parties benefit. Soul benefits.

Now the Essence of Power given to the Caring Ones serves

two different purposes. One is to work upon that area of Lands to put it in a good way for the residing beings to use – the other is to form a wall of Power, a barrier to keep out the Invaders. There is only one way in which to put Power in such a form as to withstand attack and to maintain its position and shape – *Malgum*.

The Essence of Malgum has been added to the Power substance of the containing wall, and this has a holding and sustaining effect upon that block of Power. Whilst Power contains a sufficient quantity of Malgum to hold it in shape – no substance can work upon it to change it or move it. Even beings are substance.

The Essence of the Core of the Lands of Soul is given freely to assist the Caring Ones, for their system of power is not of the same calibre as that of Soul, and cannot withstand the Invaders indefinitely. But the Essence is not given at random, for it is given only to those beings who have evolved in a way of caring and who use all for the benefit of all.

We have many allies who have joined with us, many who rely on the Essence of the Core.

We could take over their areas of Lands and incorporate them into our way of being, our way of Power and Intelligence – but such would be encroaching and against the way of Soul, of the Mass.

It is important never to encroach unless harm is being done to one who has absolutely no defence against a brutish force – and even then the encroachment should only be temporary until the other is able to stand firm in caring – alone. We will *not* try to incorporate the Caring Ones of the Aliens into our way of being – but we will *help them to become greater in their own way*, for wanting power over another is equivalent to needing that being, and we have need of no-one. Such wise and caring ones are the Controlling Intelligences of those aliens whom we assist.

The Core of all Power stands for such a way of *freedom* as man has never contemplated in this life of his, on Earth. In his true sense, in Reality, he is as I. He is as the Core of Power – *serene*.

Serenity to man is in someone slow-moving and saying little or nothing – but serenity in truth is *Peace* – doing all and, at times, communicating all.

That is *serenity* – Peace in doing, Calmness in the saying.

As there is no means of communicating with the evil Invaders, as there is within them not one spark of caring or hope of changing in any way, and because they would eventually destroy all others in their path – the Mass has no alternative but to go against them and wipe them from existence once and for all.

Now, over the hill, are our allies, the aliens of other dimensions, and beyond our very own boundaries of Power are the ever-persistent Mindless Ones.

Now is the time to go forward. Now our allies await our promised assistance, but they cannot hold out as they are much longer.

Only one obstacle prevents us from doing what must be done, for the continued existence of billions of Universes of Soul, and of many others outside of ourselves. *That obstacle is the way of man on this Earth.*

It is first necessary to clear the blockage of the flow of Power from a million Universes, Power which is required for a noble purpose.

The way of man is the cause of this blockage. It cannot be allowed to continue any longer. Either the Soul of this Universe will be fulfilled by the means of man doing his task, or the Universe will be collapsed and folded in.

Man must choose. Soul allows free choice – right up to the end – if *the end* is what man chooses.

ORISSOR ...
IS THE WAY FOR ALL

by Dorothy Fosbrooke   Price £1.

This book sets out, in a way, the outline of what would not seem right to man in his present frame of mind, but is in reality correct in every detail.

It states fact as fact has never been stated before, but whether Man chooses to believe or not is his free choice.

It speaks of the way of the organs of the body, and states factors that have never before come from the ways of the Medical Men.
You need never have cancer.

It shows how education is indoctrinating Man into something he should not be – uninspired.

It shows where fear and emotion come from, and it gives an alternative way to all factors it condemns.

Available from Booksellers and Newsagents or direct from the Publishers, post free.

THE GOLDEN AGE OF ENLIGHTENMENT – IS HERE

by Bill Dawson   Price 85p.

One spark can make a forest fire. One spark of pure Truth can set the World alight with Understanding of all things.

What is contained in this book can be that spark, for it brings Wisdom from **outside** of this Universe of yours, to bear on the real-life problems of Mankind.

Knowledge of eradicating **all** the illnesses and disorders of Man, quickly and simply, is contained within.

Illnesses of body and troubles of mind. Knowledge of the World and Universe around you. Knowledge of other Universes and the Beings who inhabit them.

It brings you knowledge of the Aliens who walk among you now, whom you do not recognise – as yet.

The Being from the Core of All Power and Intelligence enlightens you on how to use Pure Thought, and contact your own Higher Intelligence – easily.

But all this is only for those with courage to face the new Age of Enlightenment which is now being kindled.

Are you one of them?

Available from Booksellers and Newsagents, or direct from the Publishers, post free.

WOULD YOU BELIEVE AN ALIEN?

by Keith D. Edmunds   Price 85p.

Truth. Who knows where or in what direction it lies? What can Man know of Truth, when he is not even aware of his own purpose in Life?

Much has been expounded about the ways and sayings of Jesus – yet not one of those who wrote the words ever heard one word from his lips. So much for Truth!

Truth. Man has listened far too long to those who would misinform him for their own prestige.

Why not start out now to understand what all is about in you own Universe?

Know without doubt – who you are – and what you are.

I have been here before in many guises, always with the intention of putting to rights the uncaring ways of others for their Earth. But as always, you of Man have had to make your own decision – whether to believe me or not.

In this book I tell you a little of those past times. Some of you may even recall the action of them. You would then understand my way.

MY UNIVERSE WAS INVADED

by J. B. Phillips   Price £1.

Substance requires understanding – even Gold is not understood by Man, for he has no idea of how it came into being, nor what its present properties can achieve for the lifetime of Man.

Lifestyles of this era of this civilisation list Gold as precious, and do not even mention the most precious substance that is in this Universe for Man to use.

The Economy of Gold rules the lives of Man, and his Society presents the Laws that keep him hidebound to this Earth.

Why not understand what substances are at your disposal?

Invasion of a Universe by beings of such ways of mindlessness, caused my wondrous Soulparts to have to be annihilated from their home.

Soon they are to be reborn, and within these pages are many items of how all came about, and how all now takes on a way of betterment. That betterment I want to share with you of Mankind, and bring this Earth into a great way of understanding what all is about.

Available from Booksellers and Newsagents, or direct from the Publishers, post free.

NEVER BEYOND UNDERSTANDING

by Keith D. Edmunds   Price 85p.

You are here on Earth for a definite purpose.
You can understand what that purpose is.

Within these pages is information of many ways –
ways of thoughts and senses, and how your Universe
truly functions as one of many other Universes.

Past, Present and Future are herein.

Ways of putting the mind at ease. Ways of
clearing once and for all time, from the face of your
Earth, the ailments of Man.

Make sure you understand the contents, and be
sure to ask if you are in doubt.

Before every messenger, there have been pioneers
– pioneers who paved the way for that messenger.

Pioneers are now upon your Earth – and you will
see them so very soon.

YOUTH...FROM STRAIGHT-JACKET TO GLORY

by Graham Phillips   Price 85p.

Now is the time that Youth can lead the World, for a new Force is entering this Universe of yours, a Force which allies itself with the Youth of this Age.

A new era has arrived – an era of knowledge about your Earth and Universe – practical knowledge that can put every single problem and disease of the whole of Mankind to rights, and set aside the ways of Drugs and Indoctrinations.